OUR EARTH

DERRYDALE BOOKS

New York

CONTENTS

How Did the Earth Begin?

How did our world begin? Where did it come from? In ancient times, people made up imaginative stories about the beginning of the earth, but these did not really explain what had happened.

Some people were not satisfied with these stories. They watched, or observed, the skies carefully. They had no telescopes, but they could observe many things without telescopes. They saw that all the stars moved through the night sky as a group, as if they were tied together. They also saw that a few objects seemed to wander among the stars. They called these objects 'planets', which comes from a Greek word meaning 'wanderer'.

The earth is part of the solar system—the system of the sun. The moon and the other planets and their moons also belong to the solar system. The sun is at the center, and the planets move round the sun in paths called orbits. The third planet, counting outwards from the sun, is the earth.

We want to know how the earth began. To find out, we must first learn something about the beginning, or origin, of the solar system. Scientists have given several explanations, or theories, of how this might have happened. But nobody knows for sure.

AN EARLY THEORY

One of the first of these theories was proposed by the great French astronomer and mathematician Pierre Laplace in 1796. It is called the nebular hypothesis. (A hypothesis is a guess that is based on facts and does not conflict with them.) *Nebula* is the Latin word for 'cloud'; the universe contains many *nebulae*, or clouds, made up of gas and dust.

Laplace believed that the sun was once a rotating cloud of hot gas. The rotation caused the cloud to become round, like a huge ball. As the ball cooled, the cloud shrank in size and started to spin faster. (A spinning skater spins faster, too, if he reduces his size by pulling in his arms.) The shrinking and spinning caused the ball to bulge at the equator and flatten out at the poles. A ring of gas and dust then formed round the equator. This ring of material broke away from the ball, and the pieces joined together to form a planet. This planet orbited round the rest of the cloud. Meanwhile, the cloud went on shrinking and spinning faster and faster, producing more rings, each of them breaking away and forming a planet. Finally, a family of planets moving round a central globe of hot gas—the sun—was produced. This explanation seemed so reasonable that for a time everyone believed that this was how the earth and its sister planets began.

As more facts were discovered about the sun and the planets, the Laplace theory began to lose favor. The main problem was the fact that the sun spins slowly. If Laplace's theory were true, it would spin quickly. Possibly the sun had somehow slowed down, but no one could explain how this could have happened. So astronomers had to start all over again and look for new theories.

THE LITTLE PLANETS THEORY

About 1900, Thomas Chamberlin and Forest Moulton, two American scientists, put forward a new idea. It was called the planetesimal theory. ('Planetesimal' means 'little planet'.) Some years later, two British scientists, Sir James Jeans and Harold Jeffreys, proposed another theory called the tidal theory. There were some differences between the British and American theories, but the main principle was the same. At first, according to these theories, the sun had no planets. Then,

ages ago, it came very close to another star. Each body exerted its pull of gravity on the other. This raised tidal waves of hot gas which swirled round the sun and the star. As they passed each other, streams of gas were pulled out into space between the two bodies. As these two bodies moved apart, some of the streams of gas condensed to form planets.

These, too, looked like very good theories. But astronomers have had to discard them. For one thing, the passing star could not have given the planets enough motion to keep them in orbit round the sun. They would have fallen into the sun and been burned up. Also, both theories were based on the chance of a star having passed close to the sun.

The Laplace Theory: (1) The ring of gas separates from the ball of gas at the equator. (2) The material in the ring joins together to form a planet. (3) The cloud continues to spin and shrink, forming the family of planets which rotate round the sun.

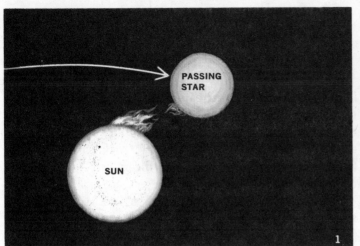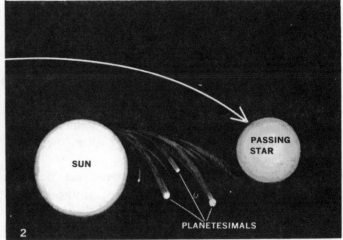

The Planetesimal Theory: (1) A passing star raises tides on the surface of the sun.
(2) Some of the streams of gases form planetesimals which become the planets.

THE DUST-CLOUD THEORY

Astronomers have since proposed more theories about the origin of the earth. All of these theories are of two main kinds. The natural, or evolutionary, theories suggest that planets form round a star as the star is created, or they form as part of its normal life. Laplace's nebular hypothesis is of this kind. Other theories are called catastrophic theories. Such theories say that planets are created round a star only by an accident or a catastrophe, such as the approach of another star or a collision with it. The planetesimal theory is of this kind.

It is important which kind of theory is correct. If a natural theory is right, most stars should have planets. But if a catastrophic theory is the explanation of how the world began, then the creation of our planet and the life on it was a very unusual event in the history of the universe. Stars are so far apart that an accident involving two stars must be very rare. In fact, during the lifetime of the solar system—which is 4,600,000,000 years—only one in every 10,000,000,000 stars could have gained planets in this way.

Astronomers can in fact detect planets around other stars. They cannot see them through their telescopes because the stars are so far away. But the planets disturb the motion of the stars and this motion can be seen. A natural theory is therefore much more likely than a catastrophic one. In fact, Laplace's nebular hypothesis is now thought to be correct in outline.

Most astronomers now believe that the sun and planets were formed from a spinning cloud of gas and dust. This theory was first developed by the German astronomer Carl von Weizsäcker in the 1940s. Since then, other astronomers have added to his theory, which is called the dust-cloud theory.

Throughout the universe there are huge clouds of dust and gas. More than 5,000,000,000 years ago, according to this theory, a large number of dust particles within such a cloud began to condense and form a globule. The particles were pulled towards the center of the globule mostly because of their mutual gravitation. As the globule became round, like a ball, it began to spin. This spinning caused it to flatten out. The center of the disc, was spinning more slowly than the outer parts. It began to condense even more. Eventually, the energy released by this process caused the temperature and the pressure in the globule to become so high that thermo-nuclear processes began. The star—our sun—then began to shine in its own right.

HOW DID THE EARTH BEGIN?

The outer parts of the dust cloud were spinning too fast to condense into one mass. They broke up into smaller, swirling masses of gas and dust, which condensed to form planets.

While our solar system was being formed over a period of millions of years, other parts of that huge cloud of gas and dust were condensing into other stars.

WHAT THE EARTH WAS LIKE

What was the newly formed earth like? Was it a ball of red-hot glowing rock? Was it cold? Or was it perhaps liquid? These questions are of great importance to geologists who study the earth.

Most geologists now agree on a general picture of the young earth. The earth formed as dust particles gathered together in a cloud in space. The particles attracted each other by gravity, so that a mass of particles collected together and formed a solid globe. As the force of gravity of the globe pulled in more and more particles, the new world grew larger and larger.

As the earth grew, it was not very hot. Its temperature was probably about the same as boiling water (100 °C). But today the inside of the earth has a much higher temperature. It is now so hot that the rock there is molten and flows from volcanoes in fiery and deadly rivers of lava.

How did the earth get so hot? There were probably several reasons for the heating of the young earth. The material of which the earth is made contains radio-active elements such as uranium. These elements are constantly producing heat—enough, in fact, to keep the center of the earth as hot as it is now. This might seem to explain how the interior of the young solid earth became molten. But the study of rocks shows that this melting happened more quickly than can be explained by radio-activity alone.

As the new planet grew, solid particles would have rained down upon its surface. The impact of each one would have produced a little heat—enough perhaps to heat the world so that its interior began to melt. Then, enough heat would have been gained by radio-activity to keep the interior hot when the bombardment of particles stopped.

The Dust-Cloud Theory: The dust-cloud (left) becomes round and begins to spin. The central mass (right) becomes the sun. The outer parts condense to form planets.

WHERE THE MOON CAME FROM

One event that did not disturb the surface of our young world was the formation of the moon. Many astronomers once thought that the moon came from the earth. Some even suggested that the Pacific Ocean covered that hole that remained when the moon left the earth. But the Apollo moon landings settled this argument. The moon is different enough from the earth to show that it was never part of the earth. The moon is about the same age as the earth—4,600,000,000 years. So it probably formed as a separate body like the earth and other planets, only to be captured later by the earth.

Mars probably captured its two moons, but it is likely that the four large outer planets made their own moons. This may have happened to all of them in much the same way as the planets were themselves formed, from the cloud of gas and dust.

HOW SPECIAL IS THE EARTH?

There are many clouds of gas and dust scattered throughout the universe. Astronomers believe that stars and planets are forming there just as our solar system formed long ago. They also believe that other planets with some form of life must exist somewhere far away in the universe.

It is impossible to guess how many planets contain life. But in case you may be thinking that our world is a special one in the universe, keep this in mind: the earth is just one of nine planets circling the sun; and the sun is just one of 100,000,000,000 stars that make up the great island of stars called the Milky Way, or the Galaxy.

Astronomers believe that they can detect about 1,000 stars which have planets, but these are only nearby stars. Possibly, almost all of the stars in the Galaxy have planets. And, as if this were not enough to think about, our most powerful telescopes can locate the distant gleam of about 1,000,000,000 other galaxies in the universe. Therefore, the total number of planets in the universe is probably many millions of millions of millions.

The small dark spots seen in the clouds of this nebula may be the beginning of new stars.

9

What the Earth is Made of

Scientists have explored almost every part of the earth's surface. They have mapped it and measured it. They have launched space ships and satellites which send back information about the earth's surface and atmosphere. As a result, we know a great deal about the surface of our planet and about its atmosphere. We know less about the interior of the earth, for it is very difficult to study. The deepest mines go about 2 miles (3.2 kilometers) below the earth's surface. Yet from where we stand to the center of the earth is nearly 4,000 miles (6,437 kilometers).

THE LAYERS OF THE PLANET

The earth is made up of many layers of different materials. Completely surrounding the solid earth and held there by its gravity is a blanket of gases. We call this the atmosphere, or air sphere. Near the ground, the gases are about 80 per cent nitrogen and 20 per cent oxygen. There is also a little argon, carbon dioxide and other gases, and water vapor. This mixture of gases is called air. The blanket of air gets thinner as it stretches upwards. The upper atmosphere has gases lighter than air. As we go higher and higher it

The earth's layers are the atmosphere (air), lithosphere (rock) and hydrosphere (water).

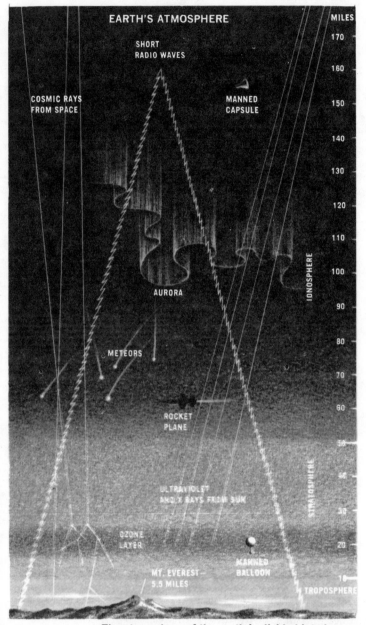

EARTH'S ATMOSPHERE

SHORT
RADIO WAVES

COSMIC RAYS
FROM SPACE

MANNED
CAPSULE

MILES
170
160
150
140
130
120
110
100
90
80
70
60
50
40
30
20
10

IONOSPHERE

AURORA

METEORS

ROCKET
PLANE

STRATOSPHERE

ULTRAVIOLET
AND X RAYS FROM SUN

OZONE
LAYER

MANNED
BALLOON

MT. EVEREST
5.5 MILES

TROPOSPHERE

The atmosphere of the earth is divided into layers.

gets thinner and thinner. It is difficult to say how thick the atmosphere is. It fades away rather than comes to a definite end. There are almost no gases left above 100 miles (160 kilometers).

Covering 70 per cent of the surface of the earth, to an average depth of 2.25 miles (3.6 kilometers), there is a thin layer of water. This is called the hydrosphere, or water sphere. If the surface of the earth were perfectly smooth, without a wrinkle or a bulge, then the seas would completely cover the earth. There would be no land. However, the rocky skeleton of the earth has high and low areas. The water has collected in the hollows; the higher parts, which are not covered by the water, form the land. Large regions of land are called continents. Small areas that rise above the water are called islands. The greatest known ocean depth is 7 miles (11.3 kilometers), whereas the highest mountain rises 5.5 miles (8.9 kilometers).

There is some water on land, too, in lakes and rivers and in tiny holes in the rocks. This water falls as rain or snow and most of it is always finding its way gradually to the sea. There the sun's heat turns some into water vapor which rises into the air. The water vapor in the air then forms rain or snow. But some water does not get to the sea. It is sucked up by plants, drunk by animals and people, or evaporated from the earth by the heat of the sun.

The solid portion of the earth is called the lithosphere, or rock sphere. We can see and touch the rocks at the surface, but we can also find out something about the rocks that are deep inside the earth. The earth is split up into several layers; each layer is lighter than the one below it. Below the light gases of the upper atmosphere are the heavier gases of the air. Below that is the water, which is heavier than air. Now we find that the rock is also in layers. The light-weight rocks are near the surface and the heavier rocks are further down. The light-weight rocks form the earth's crust, and the heavier ones form the mantle.

LEARNING ABOUT THE EARTH

Drilling into the ground to a depth greater than the height of the highest mountain is a marvellous feat. But the center of the earth is 500 times deeper than the deepest shaft. Therefore the rocks brought up by the drill will not tell us much about the inside of the earth. Volcanoes pour out molten rock from regions deeper underground, and geologists now know that in some places the rock at the earth's surface has come from deep inside. These rocks tell us more about the earth.

But scientists have not gained all their knowledge of the earth by looking at rocks. Much has been found out by studying earthquakes. When an earthquake shakes the land, vibrations spread out through the earth. This is rather like the way people living in houses built along main roads can sometimes feel the vibrations of heavy trucks passing outside. Earthquake vibrations (scientists call them seismic waves) pass right through the earth. They can still be noticed thousands of miles from the earthquake itself. The waves are very, very weak when they arrive, but sensitive instruments called seismographs can pick them up. With the help of computers, scientists can tell where the waves have come from and what has happened to them on the way. In this way, we are able to get information about the inside of the earth.

Seismic waves behave differently depending on the kind of rock through which they pass. Some kinds of waves will not go through molten rock, which muffles them. In solid, heavy rock the waves move more quickly than in light rock. By studying seismic waves, scientists have been able to tell which kinds of rock make up the different layers of the earth's interior.

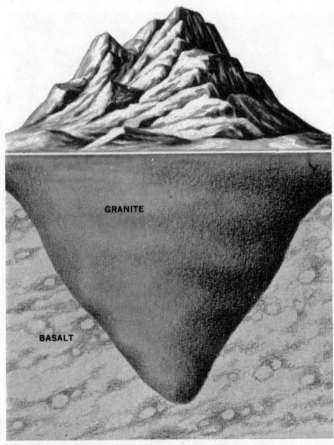

The top layer of the earth's crust is mainly made of granite. A heavier rock, basalt, lies below.

The Earth's Crust

The outermost layer of rock is known as the earth's crust. We live on top of a few yards or meters of soil covering the crust. The depth of the crust varies. Under the continents it is about 20 miles (32 kilometers) thick. But under the ocean-bed it is much thinner—only about 6 miles (10 kilometers). Earthquake waves travel quite slowly through the crust. But at the bottom of the crust they suddenly begin to move quickly. This change in the speed of the waves shows that they have entered a new layer of heavier rocks, called the mantle. The boundary between the two layers is called the Mohorovičić Discontinuity, after the Yugoslav scientist who discovered it. This name is rather difficult to say, so it is usually just called moho. In the 1960s, American scientists tried to drill a hole down to the moho. This experiment was called the Mohole Project. In 1966 it was abandoned by the United States government before it was completed.

The crust is made of light rocks mainly containing the elements oxygen, silicon, aluminium and iron. These elements are combined in many different ways to make different kinds of rocks. Sand, for example, is made up of oxygen and silicon. Clay is made up of oxygen, silicon and aluminium.

The Mantle

As we get deeper underground, it gets hotter and the pressure increases. The high pressure makes the rocks denser, or heavier. Scientists try to find out what rocks are like deep underground by squeezing minerals in powerful machines that can produce very great pressure. They have tested all kinds of minerals. In this way they have found out which kinds probably lie deep in the earth. The mantle is thought to be made up of a mineral called olivine, which contains oxygen, silicon, magnesium and iron.

The mantle stretches down for 1,780 miles (2,865 kilometers) beneath the crust. It has several layers, but the most interesting are the top two layers just below the crust. Both layers are about 60 miles (97 kilometers) deep. The first is completely solid, but the second is half solid and half liquid and is probably rather slushy. The top layer is split up into a group of plates lying beneath the crust.

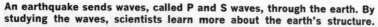

An earthquake sends waves, called P and S waves, through the earth. By studying the waves, scientists learn more about the earth's structure.

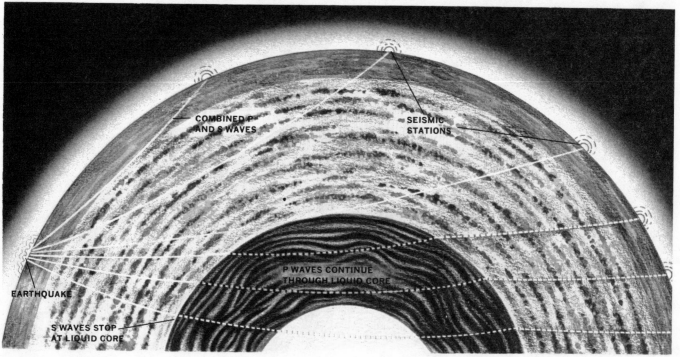

COMBINED P AND S WAVES

SEISMIC STATIONS

P WAVES CONTINUE THROUGH LIQUID CORE

EARTHQUAKE

S WAVES STOP AT LIQUID CORE

The plates carry the crust and can move about over the slushy layer which separates them from the rest of the solid mantle.

The Earth's Core

Underneath the mantle, some kinds of seismic waves stop. They cannot push any further because the next layer, the outer core, is liquid. Scientists think the liquid is mainly a mixture of molten iron and nickel. Meteorites that fall to earth from space are made of these metals. It is likely that they are made of a similar mixture of metals as the outer core. But pure iron and nickel are heavier than the material of the outer core. So there must be another element in the core. Most geologists think that this other element is silicon.

The outer core is 1,400 miles (2,253 kilometers) deep. Below, stretching another 760 miles (1,223 kilometers) down to the center of the earth, is a solid inner core. No one knows what the inner core is made of. Possibly it is solid iron and nickel, which solidified under great pressure. Here, in the heart of the earth, the temperature may be as much as 4000 °C (10400 °F).

HOW THE LAYERS FORMED

Most geologists think that the earth had a cold start. It began as a ball of rock made from rock particles in space. This rock was a mixture of materials. There would have been no oceans or blankets of air round it. But as the earth's interior grew hotter from the radio-activity of its minerals, the earth began to change. The rocks began to sort themselves out: the heavier materials moved down to the center of the earth and the lighter rocks rose to the surface. Gradually the crust and the other layers formed. Volcanoes began to erupt in violent bursts of fire all over the earth. Gases came rushing out, and these formed an atmosphere. Just which gases made up earth's first atmosphere no one knows for certain. However, they included water vapor, which condensed to give liquid water. The oceans began to form and become salty as they dissolved salt from the rocks. But the early atmosphere contained no oxygen. Somehow the first traces of oxygen began to appear, perhaps as sunlight broke up water vapor and released the oxygen. Once oxygen was in the atmosphere, some form of life could start to develop. Plants gave out oxygen, and as more and more of them grew the oxygen in the atmosphere increased. But this happened very slowly. The air as we know it today was not completely formed until about 20,000,000 years ago.

The crust, mantle and inner core of the earth are solid. The outer core is made of a molten liquid.

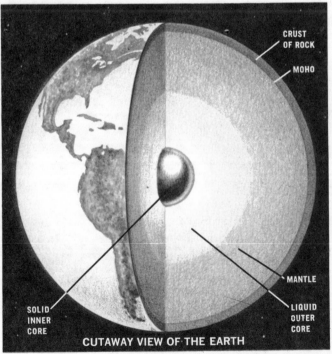

CUTAWAY VIEW OF THE EARTH

CRUST OF ROCK

MOHO

MANTLE

LIQUID OUTER CORE

SOLID INNER CORE

'It's as solid as a rock!', we often say, as we proudly show how firm a piece of our handiwork is. By this we mean that what we have built is so strong and so sturdy it will last forever. Now we might ask, 'How solid is a rock? How long does it last?'

Most of the earth is made of rock. On the surface, mountains and canyons, hills and valleys, steep cliffs and flat plains cover the land. Under the sea, great ridges and trenches cross the ocean floor. All these features are made of rock. But are these features the same as when the earth was formed? Will they be the same in the future? The answer is 'No'. Nothing on earth—not even solid rock—lasts forever, because we live on a planet that is always changing.

If you leave footprints on a sandy beach, you probably won't be able to find them the next day. The tide will have washed them away, or the wind will have blown the sand smooth. But the astronauts' footprints on the moon will last for millions of years, because the moon is a dead, unchanging world.

Why are the earth and moon so different? One of the main reasons is that the earth has air and water but the moon is airless and dry. Air and water work all the time on the earth to wear down mountains and fill up valleys. But before we find out how this happens let us see how mountains are formed.

The 'Dancing Girls', part of the West Macdonnel Range in Australia seen from the air, clearly shows mountains formed by folds in the rock.

RAISING THE ROCKS

At the top of the highest mountains, geologists have found *fossils* (hardened remains) of animals that lived in the sea a long time ago. When the animals died, they sank to the sea bed and became part of the rock there. Then, great forces from the center of the earth pushed the rocks from the sea floor high into the air. In many places, the forces slowly squeezed the ends of large sections of rock together, so that they

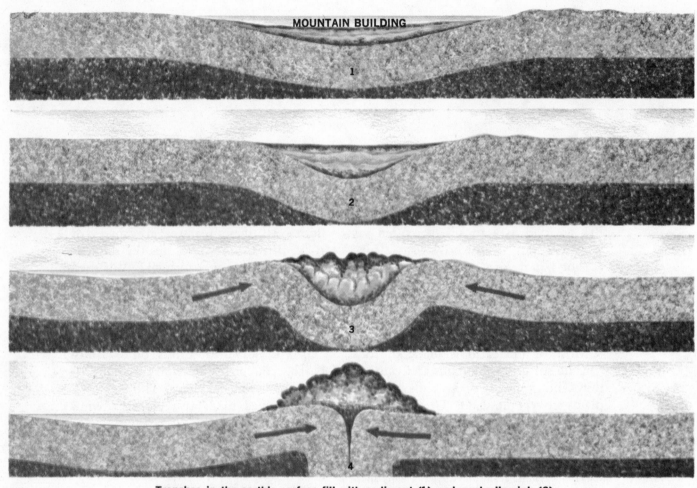

**Trenches in the earth's surface fill with sediment (1) and gradually sink (2).
Pressure squeezes the rock (3) and forces it upwards into a mountain range (4).**

buckled up into folds. The folds became mountains and valleys.

Rock is made up of layers called *strata*, and folds occur where the layers bend. Sometimes you can see these folds clearly when you look at a mountain from a great distance or from the air. Small folds, looking like wrinkles, can sometimes be seen in cliffs. Those that fold upwards, like a *U* upside-down, are called *anticlines*. As the rocks fold, parallel ranges of hills or gentle mountains and valleys are formed. If the squeezing continues, the folds may begin to topple over each other. This makes rugged mountains, such as the Alps of central Europe.

Rock, then, is obviously not completely solid if it can be treated in this way. If great pressure is put on it, it will usually bend and stretch. But sometimes it holds firm, and will eventually snap under pressure. When this happens, there occurs what we call an 'earthquake'. Most earthquakes, even those that cause great damage, are produced by only small movements of rock. Such a break in the rock is called a *fault*. The strata slip out of line on either side of a fault, like the join between two pieces of wallpaper that do not match properly.

One side of a fault may be pushed over the other. Mountains are also built

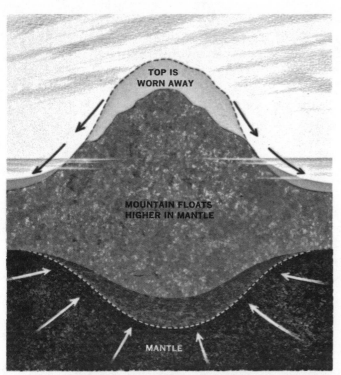

TOP IS
WORN AWAY

MOUNTAIN FLOATS
HIGHER IN MANTLE

MANTLE

Erosion wears down a mountain over a long period
of time. The mountain becomes lighter and slowly
rises because it is floating higher in the mantle.

building is a long and slow one. We cannot see mountains being formed because the movements are far too slow. But we can detect fault movements, which may amount to a few centimeters a year. Scientists can reproduce folding in the laboratory by squeezing layers of clay or other substances.

But we can often watch another kind of mountain building, and it is a spectacular sight. This is the action of volcanoes. When a volcano erupts, it pours out *lava*, molten rock which solidifies to form new rock. In this way a new mountain is born.

This happened with the Mexican volcano, Paricutín, in 1943. On 20 February, it erupted in a field. The next morning, a smoking cone 25 feet (7·5 meters) high stood in the field. Within a week, the volcano was 550 feet (170 meters) high. When the eruption finally finished nine years later, Paracutín had risen to a height of 9,100 feet (2,780 meters)!

Some of the world's highest mountains were formed by volcanic action. They can often be distinguished from other mountains because they are shaped like cones.

up in this way. The great Sierra Nevada of California is made up of a huge block of rock that broke loose in the earth's crust millions of years ago, and was forced up into a mountain range.

Faults may occur where the rock has been pulled apart. Where there are two faults close to each other, the block of rock between them may sink. This produces a steep-sided valley called a *rift valley*.

Slow and Sudden Changes

Folding and faulting often occur together. Mountains made by folding often have faults in various places. Fault-block mountains will also show folds here and there. Except for the sudden violence of an earthquake when a fault occurs, the process of mountain-

WEARING THE ROCKS AWAY

We know how mountains appeared on the earth's surface millions of years ago. But what about the other features such as plains, gorges and caves? How did they come to be? Obviously, there must have been other influences at work besides the powerful mountain-building forces. These other influences shaped the land by gradually wearing it away. This natural wearing process is called *erosion*, and it includes the forces of *glaciers* (moving rivers of ice), running water, waves and wind.

Erosion is a very slow process. Usually, we cannot see erosion actually happening, even if we spend all our lives in one place. But it is at work in every muddy river, in every cloud of dust, and in the waves that crash against the seashore. One important factor in erosion—heat—is felt rather than seen.

During the day, the warmth of the sun causes rock surfaces to expand. At night, these surfaces cool and contract. This daily change in temperature does not spread far down inside the rocks. But although it is very, very small, the constant expansion and contraction eventually produces cracks in the surface. During winter, water seeps into the cracks and freezes. In doing so, it expands in volume and opens the cracks a little wider. Eventually the solid rocks slowly crumble into particles of soil and dust.

Water Washes Away

Rivers and streams flowing down rocky hillsides always carry some soil away with them. Sometimes the water washes away all the soil and leaves rock exposed to the sun, wind and rain. The rock never stops breaking up, and the river carves out a channel in the hillside. This action is very slow, but it is going on all the time. The channel gets deeper and deeper as the river carries away more soil. Little streams join the river, or it joins a larger river. Slowly many valleys begin to cut through the range of hills.

As the rivers reach the land at the foot of the hills, they begin to flow more slowly. The soil in the water begins to settle on the bottom. Gradually, the low-lying land fills with soil and forms a plain. Rivers wind slowly over the plain. Hollows fill with water

Coastlines are constantly changing through the process of water erosion.

and form lakes. The river water absorbs carbon dioxide gas from the air. This makes the water slightly acid. Some rocks, especially limestone, are affected by acid and worn down. In those places where there is limestone or similar rock, the rivers sometimes carve out deep gorges and caves by this wearing-away process. This kind of erosion is called *chemical erosion*.

Wind and Ice Grind into Dust

Water has other helpers in shaping the land. The wind can also carry away soil and dust from rocks. Rock particles carried by the wind will strike another rock and grind it down. If we stand on the beach on a windy day we can feel the tiny grains of sand in the wind stinging our bare skin. Think of what thousands of years of such bombardment does to the land. The grains of soil and sand carried by the wind eventually fall to the ground and settle. They collect in hollows and low-lying regions, building up the soil.

Ice is another rock-breaker. Glaciers drag huge boulders with them as they slowly creep down the hillsides and mountain slopes. This leaves broad valleys behind them, carved out of the land. Valleys formed by glaciers are *U*-shaped. A river valley is *V*-shaped, because the river always cuts the land away at the lowest point of the valley.

The Waves of the Sea Invade

The great undersea ridges and trenches were made by the same forces that made the mountains on land. But the sea floor is eroded by different forces from those that work on land. Sand, mud and shells collect on the sea bed and form and change its surface. But the sea itself erodes the land. Waves and tides cut deep into the seashore, pounding away at beaches and attacking cliffs. Cliff erosion can be very rapid. As the waves continue their battering, pieces of rock fall into the sea. Gradually, the cliff face is cut back into the land. People may have to abandon their cliff-top houses. People in seaside towns try to stop erosion of the shore by building breakwaters and sea walls.

The action of the sea is relentless, slowly changing coastlines round the world. In many places, the cutting action is reversed. Sand or soil carried into the sea by rivers, or moved by currents in the sea, builds up on the shore. Gradually, the land extends into the sea. In south-east England, there are several towns that were sea ports in the Middle Ages. But now they lie 2 miles (3 kilometers) inland.

THE EVER-CHANGING LAND

This erosion wears down the earth's surface. Slowly, over thousands or millions of years, mountains have become hills and hills have become plains. But, if erosion has been going on for so long, why is the land not smooth and flat everywhere? During the earth's long life, there would have been plenty of time for this to happen.

The answer is that the earth's surface is also constantly changing from below. Erosion may wear down a mountain, but forces inside the earth push another mountain up, either in the same place or elsewhere. These ceaseless movements are going on right now, in all parts of the earth. And they will continue to do so for as long as the earth remains a living planet.

Although erosion is usually a smoothing agent, in some places it makes the land less smooth. This is because some parts of the land or coast are made of a mixture of soft rock and hard rock. Erosion wears away the soft rock, leaving a column or block of hard rock exposed. Offshore clumps of rock form in this way, and so do the strange stone pinnacles of some moorlands and deserts. The sides of the Grand Canyon have 'steps' of hard rock.

But the Grand Canyon owes its great depth not just to erosion alone. Part of the land that it cuts through has risen steadily for millions of years. This double action of cutting away and up-building keeps the Colorado River flowing swiftly several thousand feet down.

Plant growth slows erosion down. The plant roots hold the soil together and prevent it from being washed or blown away. Farmers who wish to protect their land make sure that they grow trees, bushes and grass for that purpose. Once erosion starts, it is difficult to stop, and the continual loss of soil discourages new growth.

In the Mediterranean region, there were once great forests where there are now dry, bare stretches of land. This has happened because men cut down the forests and allowed their goats and other grazing animals to eat up the plants.

Tennyson, in his well-known poem *The Brook,* wrote a line that expresses perfectly the slow shaping of the land by nature. He quotes the babbling brook as saying: 'For men may come and men may go, but I go on forever.'

Grand Canyon, Arizona: erosion has cut away the soft rock, leaving the hard rock exposed.

20

The Ever-Changing Earth

If you had lived on a distant planet and had visited the earth millions of years ago, what would our world have looked like to you? As you looked at the earth from space, would you have seen the Americas on one side of the world, Australia on the other and Antarctica covered by ice at the southern pole?

If your visit had taken place 100,000,000 years ago, you would have seen a very different earth from that viewed by the Apollo astronauts on their way to and from the moon. You would have seen that the Americas were in two separate pieces. North America was near Europe, and South America lay close to Africa. Not far away, on the other side of Africa, Australia and Antarctica were joined together.

If you had visited the earth 200,000,000 years ago, you would have seen just one huge super-continent made up of all today's continents joined together. On the other side of the earth, you would

Millions of years ago the continents were joined together in a single mass.

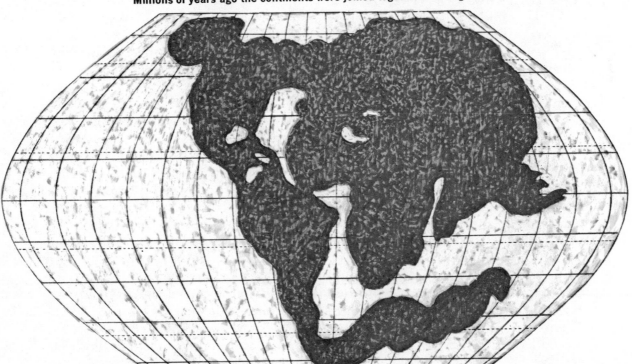

not have seen any land at all.

The face of the earth has been constantly changing during its lifetime. The continents have slowly drifted into different positions. Sometimes they have joined together to form large super-continents, and then broken into smaller pieces. This process is still going on. But it is happening so slowly that the map of the world will not have to be drawn again for a very long time.

Immense forces inside the earth are pulling and pushing whole continents around the globe like pieces on a gigantic chessboard. Experts believe that these same forces also cause mountains to rise, volcanoes to erupt and earthquakes to shake the earth. When you remember that the land is also constantly being eroded, or worn away, you can see that the earth is changing all the time.

THE DRIFTING CONTINENT

In the decades following Columbus' discovery of America, the outlines of the New World were mapped. It then became obvious that the coastlines on either side of the Atlantic Ocean matched each other in shape. They looked like separate pieces of a huge jigsaw puzzle. South America could once have been joined to Africa, with the bulge of Brazil fitting closely into the Gulf of Guinea. The east coast of North America, from Florida to Newfoundland, could have fitted along the north-west coast of Africa and Spain, with Newfoundland jutting out towards the Bay of Biscay. And the way these pieces of land could have been fitted together suggested that the continents were indeed once joined. If this were so, then the Atlantic Ocean would have slowly filled up the gap as the New World and the Old World drifted apart.

But few people were willing to believe that this had actually happened. The legend of Atlantis, which suggested that the ocean formed when the mythical continent of Atlantis sank, was popular at that time. And the Bible taught that the seas were formed in a day. Nor could anyone explain how the continents could move about on an earth that seemed to be made of solid rock.

The Theory of Alfred Wegener

But, as time went by, there was more and more evidence that the continents did drift. In 1910, the German scientist Alfred Wegener (1880–1930) put forward a reasonable theory of continental drift.

Wegener drew attention to the shape of the coastlines. He also pointed out the curious fact that coal is found all over the Northern Hemisphere, where the climate is cool or cold. But coal comes from the remains of tropical plants. Wegener also claimed that many warm regions in the Southern Hemisphere showed signs that they were once covered by ice. This meant that land that is now cold must once have been warm and, similarly, land that is now warm must once have been cold. This could have happened if the earth had at one time swung round so that the poles pointed towards the sun. But scientists believe that such a movement is impossible. Wegener said that the only other way in which this could have happened was by a drifting of the continents. In other words, the land that we now find at the poles has come from the tropics, and land in the tropics was once at the poles.

Wegener went on to show where the continents had been at various times. He found fossils (hardened remains) of the same extinct animals on the Atlantic coasts of both South America and Africa. This was more evidence that the two continents were once joined together. He also showed that mountain ranges look as though they could have continued across the gap between the two continents. These matching fossils and features of the earth's crust on the coastlines of the Pacific and Indian Oceans suggested that India, Australia and Antarctica had once been joined together fitting against the east coast of Africa.

In fact, Wegener believed that all the continents had once been part of an enormous super-continent. He called this super-continent Pangaea, a name that comes from Greek words meaning 'all earth'. By working out the age of the fossils, he claimed that the continents had joined together about 200,000,000 years ago. But, in spite of all the evidence, most experts did not agree with him because nobody at that time could explain how the continents moved.

Hot rock is carried by convection currents from the interior of the earth towards the earth's surface.

CONVECTION CURRENTS IN THE EARTH

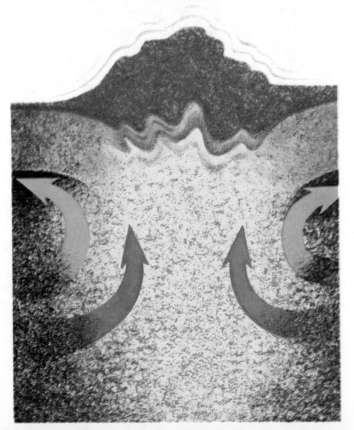

Swirling Currents Inside the Earth

Shortly after Wegener died, a British scientist named Arthur Holmes (1890–1965) tried to explain how the continents might drift. He said that the continents were like huge rafts of light rock that floated on denser rock inside the earth. Rock is normally solid, but when it gets very hot it becomes molten. So Holmes said that the rock could actually flow a few inches a year inside the earth. *Convection currents*, by which heat passes from one place to another, would carry hot rock from the very hot interior of the earth towards the surface. The currents would spread out as they reached the surface in the same way that hot currents of air rise above a radiator and spread through a room.

Holmes thought that convection currents must rise underneath the oceans and carry the floating continents slowly round the globe. Where the rock cooled, it would sink back into the earth's interior. But Holmes had no evidence to support his ideas, so the theory of continental drift was still not widely accepted. More knowledge of the earth's interior was needed. Just before Holmes died in 1965, startling new evidence was discovered which proved that his theory was correct.

Secrets of the Ocean Floor

Holmes believed that the key to continental drift lay beneath the oceans. But he could go no further until the ocean floors were mapped and their rocks analyzed. This work was not done to any great extent until the 1950s and 1960s. Then some surprising discoveries were made, especially by the American research ship *Glomar Challenger*.

First, *oceanographers* (scientists who study the ocean) discovered an enormous mountain range, or ridge, under the sea. The ridge runs the entire length of the Atlantic Ocean. It then continues south of Africa, across the Indian Ocean to the south of Australia. From there it goes right across the Pacific to the Gulf of California. It is the longest mountain range in the world, longer than the circumference of the earth itself, which is 25,000 miles (40,233 kilometers). The ridge reaches a height of 2½ miles (4 kilometers). Here and there its summits show above the waves, forming mid-ocean islands such as Iceland and Tristan da Cunha. The islands of the ridge are volcanic and often erupt.

As well as mapping the ocean floor, the research ships drilled for samples of mud and rock. They found that the layers of *sediment*—mud and other materials that settle on the ocean bed—are 2 miles (3 kilometers) thick in places. This may seem a lot, but the layers would be much thicker if sediment had been collecting on the ocean bed during the whole of the earth's lifetime. The comparative thinness of the layers shows that the oceans are much younger than the earth itself.

The research ships made another important and unexpected discovery when they tested the magnetism in the rocks of the ocean bed. This was that the direction of magnetism in the rocks varies. In 1906, a group of French scientists found that young volcanic rocks are magnetized in the same north–south direction as the earth. But when they came to test some of the older layers, they found that the rocks were magnetized in the opposite direction to the earth's magnetic field.

This strange discovery seemed to show that the earth's magnetic field was reversed in the past. At that time a com-

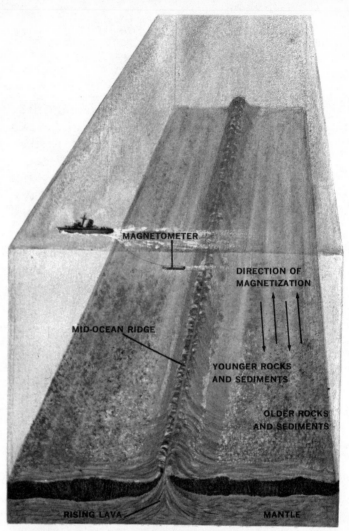

The direction of magnetism in the rocks on the ocean floor varies according to the age of the rocks.

pass needle would have pointed south instead of north. In fact, tests show that the earth's magnetic field has been reversed 12 times during the last 4,500,000 years. When such a reversal takes place, the magnetic field all over the earth changes direction.

Different Patterns of Magnetism

The ridges in the middle of the ocean are volcanic. The volcanic rocks on the ocean floor also show changes in magnetism. On land, the reversals can be detected in layers of solidified lava piled on top of each other. The rocks from the oldest lava flows lie at the bottom, and newer rocks have formed above them.

But the magnetism recorded on the sea bed shows a different pattern. There, the reversals are spread out horizontally across the ocean floor. This shows that younger rocks do not lie on top of older rocks, but alongside them. When the reversals are plotted on a map, they show up in strips. The direction of magnetization in each strip is the opposite to that of its neighbour. Each strip is a few miles wide and runs parallel to the mid-oceanic ridge. The rocks from the oldest lava flows lie furthest away from the ridge. The younger the rocks, the nearer they are to the ridge.

The pattern of strips suggests that the ocean floor is slowly spreading. It seems to be splitting into two sections at the mid-oceanic ridge. Lava rises from the inside of the earth and flows through cracks in the ridge to form new rock. This explains the volcanic nature of the mid-oceanic islands. New rock moves away from the ridge on the spreading ocean floor. Sediment taken from the sea bed shows that the further the sediment lies from the ridges, the thicker it

becomes. This is more evidence to show that the ocean floor is spreading. As the floor moves beneath the ocean, it piles up more and more sediment. This shows that the rocks furthest from the ridge are the oldest, because sediment has been collecting there far longer.

Where the Land Ends

When the edge of the ocean floor reaches a large land mass such as a continent, it rises steeply to form a *continental slope*. Then, before it reaches the coastline, it levels off into a shallow stretch of sea bed called a *continental shelf*. The continental slope marks the true boundary of a continent. In the 1960s, scientists began to use computers to make maps that showed the outlines of the continental shelves of continents, instead of showing their coastlines, as had been done before. They found that the new outlines could be matched very closely. If the ocean floor were to contract, or grow smaller, instead of spread, the continents would draw closer together until they met at their continental

The continents and the earth's crust rest on the mantle. The mantle's heat enables it to flow slowly, adjusting to the changing weight of the continents.

CONTINENTAL ROCK

SHELF

OCEAN

SEDIMENT

BASALTIC LAYER

BASE OF CRUST (MOHO)

DENSE ROCK OF MANTLE

slopes. So it seems that the continents must have been joined at their continental slopes at some time in the past.

Scientists can tell how fast the ocean floor has been spreading by counting the reversals of magnetism in the rocks. When they used this information to work out the age of the continents, they calculated that they must have all been part of one super-continent 200,000,000 years ago. Therefore Wegener's theory was correct and his Pangaea did exist.

The ocean floor also gave up other secrets. It began to give more proof that there are convection currents inside the earth. These currents would reach the earth's surface through the ridges under the sea. At the surface they would spread out, carrying the ocean floor and the continents with them. And as the ocean floor spread, so the continents would drift with it.

The experts now began to realize that a whole new theory of the structure of the earth was opening up before them. It explained many other things about the earth's crust besides continental drift. And it completely changed men's ideas about earth science during the 1960s. The theory is called *plate tectonics*.

THE MOVING PLATES

The earth's crust is not a single solid shell like the shell of an egg. Instead it is split up into at least seven large rigid plates and eight smaller ones. If a hard-boiled egg is cracked so that its shell is broken into several pieces sticking to the egg white inside, then it would look like the earth's crust. The plates are about 60 miles (97 kilometers) thick. They lie on top of a layer that is probably rather slushy. This lower layer is about as thick as the plates.

The plates move slowly about the earth at speeds of a half an inch to 4 inches (1 to 10 centimeters) a year. They do not all move in the same direction. Some plates bump into each other, some slide past each other and others move away from each other. The earth is most active at the edges of the plates, and its activity comes from their movement.

If we take a map of the world and mark on it the places where volcanoes erupt and earthquakes happen, and where the youngest mountains are, then we shall be marking out the edges of the plates. A plate may lie beneath land and ocean. The African plate, for example, carries the whole of Africa as well as the eastern half of the southern Atlantic Ocean and the western half of the Indian Ocean.

How Rifts Form

Where plates move apart, new rock rises to the surface from the earth's interior. The new rock adds itself to the edge of the plates in volcanic eruptions and earthquakes. Surtsey, the volcano that suddenly rose from the sea off Iceland in 1963, marks the place where the North American plate separated from the Eurasian plate. Where this happens beneath the oceans, a mid-oceanic ridge forms. A *rift* (steep-sided valley) runs along the very top of the ridge. The sides of the rift are the actual sides of the separating plates.

Where plates separate beneath the land, a large rift valley appears. The Red Sea is a rift valley that has been filled with water. If you look at a map of the Red Sea, you will notice that its sides are almost the same shape. They were obviously once joined together. The rifts continue northwards to the Dead Sea and southwards into the rift valleys of eastern Africa.

What Causes Volcanoes and Earthquakes?

Volcanoes and earthquakes also commonly occur where the plates move into each other. In some places the plates meet beneath the ocean, and one plate slips under the other. As it does so, it pulls the sea bed down with it, forming deep trenches in the ocean floor. The light rocks of the floor that is carried down quickly melt in the great heat of the earth's *mantle* (the inner zone below the crust) and rise back towards the surface.

This action produces volcanoes near the trench, and eventually forms chains of volcanic islands. The islands off the eastern coast of Asia, such as those that make up Japan, were formed in this way. The deepest trenches in the world's ocean also occur there. They mark the point where the Pacific plate slides under the Eurasian plate. The plate continues to be pulled down into the earth's interior. It finally breaks up at a depth of about 440 miles (708 kilometers). At that depth the rocks circulate through the earth's mantle and eventually rise to form a new plate. An ocean ridge, therefore, marks the birth of a plate, and an ocean trench marks its death.

In some places, colliding plates carry continents, not oceans. In such cases, the rock layers fold into mountain ranges, and earthquakes and volcanoes shake the land. This is happening now at the southern edge of the Eurasian plate. New peaks are being pushed up from the Atlas Mountains in North Africa right across to the Himalayas in the heart of Asia.

Some plates simply slide past each other instead of meeting or parting. Regions where this happens are called *transform faults*. The movement causes no disturbance as long as it continues steadily. But sometimes the plates stick to each other and become compressed, like a tightened spring. This may continue for years, with pressure building up all the time. Suddenly the ground gives way and the plates snap past each other. Then there is a severe earthquake.

This action is happening along the San Andreas Fault in California, where Two plates are moving past each other at a rate of 2½ inches (6 centimeters) a year.

NEW MAPS FOR OLD

What did the super-continent of Pangaea look like? Were there other continents around the world before it was formed? What will the face of the globe look like in the future? The study of plate movements can help to answer some of these questions.

Pangaea existed 200,000,000 years ago. The Americas were close to Africa and Europe. Greenland slotted in between Canada and Scandinavia, and was near Great Britain. India, Australia and Antarctica were very near to the eastern side of Africa.

When the super-continents began to break up, the Americas moved westwards, opening up the Atlantic Ocean. South America went first, and North America followed. Antarctica parted from the other side of Africa. Greenland and Europe moved northwards, and Africa and Asia swung round to meet each other, closing the Tethys Ocean. India moved northwards to meet Asia. They collided about 50,000,000 years ago, and produced the Himalayas. Australia parted from Antarctica, and the world began to look more like it does today.

It seems that continents were drifting around the globe before Pangaea was formed, and have probably been moving about for at least 2,500,000,000 years. Before Pangaea, there were three continents which were formed from the break-up of another super-continent about 500,000,000 years ago. These three were Asia; Euro-America (made up of North America, Greenland and northern Europe); and Gondwanaland (Southern Europe, Africa, South America, India, Antarctica and Australia). These three collided to form Pangaea. The super-continent lasted 40,000,000 years before breaking up. But that is not long in the history of the earth.

How Continents Move

What of the future? The plates will continue to move, slowly changing the map of the world. During your waking day, the continent on which you are living will move by about the thickness of this page. But centers of continents are not likely to be greatly affected.

These are also the centers of the plates, and are made up of very old rocks. They are often marked up by great plains or high plateaus.

Elsewhere mountains will continue to rise. And, as the plates collide or part, volcanoes and earthquakes will continue to cause destruction.

But geography will be different for students of the distant future. If the Atlantic and the Indian oceans continue to open as they are now doing, and the Pacific continues to close, we shall have another super-continent in about 200,000,000 years time. China, Japan and California will be at its heart, because North America will have collided with Asia. Meanwhile, the Mediterranean Sea will have closed, forcing Europe and Africa together. And in 100,000,000 years time, Australia may have reached China.

Then the world really will be a different place to live in.

The map shows six of the major plates which make up the crust of the earth.

THE EARTH'S CRUSTAL PLATES

EURASIA
EURASIA
AMERICA
PACIFIC
AFRICA
AUSTRALIA
ANTARCTIC

How Earthquakes Shake the Land

Anybody who has lived through an earthquake will never forget it. The land shakes and buildings tremble; cars collide in the streets; fires break out; trees and telegraph poles collapse; and everywhere there is panic. A bad earthquake can seem like the end of the world to the people caught in it. Most victims find themselves quite helpless in the face of this gigantic force.

Earthquakes are very common. There are 500,000 earth movements every year. But only 100,000 of them are large enough to be felt, and only 1,000 of these are big enough to cause any damage.

WHY EARTHQUAKES HAPPEN

If you hold one end of a ruler firmly on a table-top, and press the other end over the edge of the table, the ruler will bend. When you let go of the end of the ruler it will spring back, quivering rapidly several times. During an earthquake, the land behaves very much like the ruler. Great forces beneath the ground push one piece of rock past another. At first, the rocks stick together. Then, when the pressure becomes too great, the rocks give way. They snap past each other and quiver as they settle into their new positions. This new break between

Large earthquakes release gigantic forces and cause an enormous amount of damage. This picture was taken after the Alaskan earthquake in 1965.

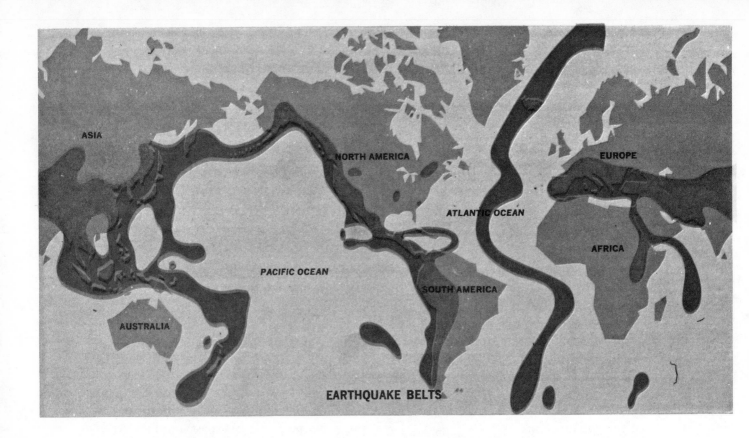

ASIA

NORTH AMERICA

EUROPE

ATLANTIC OCEAN

AFRICA

PACIFIC OCEAN

SOUTH AMERICA

AUSTRALIA

EARTHQUAKE BELTS

the rocks is called a *fault*. Sometimes the forces split a section of rock in two.

The surface of the ground shakes as the rocks spring apart. Buildings topple. Gas, water and sewage pipes crack. Electricity and telephone cables are cut, and roads break up. Fire and disease soon spread in cities ruined by earthquakes. And rescuers and medical teams often have great difficulty in reaching the area.

Even a light earthquake can kill. It does not take a very big earthquake to topple flimsy buildings. And falling bricks and woodwork can crush many people. This happened in Agadir in Morocco, where a light earthquake killed 12,000 people in 1960. But this was a small disaster compared with the results of the world's worst earthquake. It happened in China, in 1556, and claimed 830,000 lives.

WHERE EARTHQUAKES HAPPEN

There are three main earthquake belts in the world. One runs round the edges of the Pacific Ocean. Another runs down the center of the Atlantic Ocean. And the third passes from Indonesia through southern Asia to the Mediterranean Sea. In these belts, the rock beneath the ground is not firm or steady. This is because the solid part just below the earth's crust is made up of plates of rock, whose edges lie in these areas. The plates move slowly all the time, colliding, sliding past each other, or moving apart. These movements produce earthquakes at the edges of the plates.

Most earthquakes start near the earth's surface at depths of up to 15 miles (24 kilometers). But some occur deeper than this, and a few occur as deep as 440 miles (700 kilometers). The deep earthquakes are caused by plates moving down into the earth's *mantle* (the inner zone just inside the outer shell); they can trigger off earthquakes. The plates are destroyed at depths of about 440 miles (700 kilometers). This is why earthquakes do not occur deeper than this.

Many plates dive down into the earth's interior beneath the oceans. The earthquakes they cause shake the sea floor and set up waves on the surface. These waves are not very high at first, but they stretch for miles across the ocean. They travel at speeds of up to 500 miles (800 kilometers) an hour. When they approach the coast, they drag against the sea bed, and their crests rise higher and higher. The water at first runs out from the shore, leaving the sea bed bare. Then the waves rush in like a mighty wall of water. They smash against the shore, destroying everything in their path.

These waves are popularly called *tidal waves*, but they have nothing to do with the tides. The correct name for such a wave is *tsunami*—a Japanese word meaning 'harbor wave'. Tsunamis are common in the eastern Pacific.

WHEN EARTHQUAKES OCCUR

Scientists who study earthquakes are called *seismologists*. This name comes from the Greek word *seismos*, meaning earthquake. As soon as an earthquake occurs anywhere in the world, they can tell how strong it is. Seismologists can also plot its exact position. They do this with an instrument called a *seismograph*. An earthquake sends out seismic waves. These waves are rather like the waves set up in a pond when a stone is thrown into it. The water waves spread across the surface of the pond, just as seismic waves ripple through the earth.

There are two kinds of seismic waves. Primary waves, or *P* waves, are what scientists call *longitudinal*, or lengthwise, waves. When a line of railroad cars is being switched, you will notice that when the engine pushes the first car, a gap moves all the way down the line of cars. *P* waves move through rock by pushing rock particles backwards and forwards in much the same way as an engine switches cars.

Secondary waves, or *S* waves, are *transverse*, or horizontal, waves. If you take a piece of rope, tie it to a post at one end and shake the other end, you will set up transverse waves in the rope. It will move like a snake. When *S* waves travel through rock, the particles move from side to side like the coils of the rope.

When an earthquake occurs, these waves travel through the earth and are picked up at seismic stations. Seismographs contain a heavy weight hanging like a pendulum. When the seismic waves arrive, the ground shakes slightly. The quivering is not strong enough to move the heavy weight. But the other parts of the instrument feel this quivering and the movements are recorded electrically. *P* and *S* waves travel at different speeds. This means that they arrive at the seismic

The gap in the fence (below) was caused by the shifting of the earth's crust. The photographic seismograph (right) records earthquakes. An earthquake causes a coil in the magnet to move, generating an electric current that moves a mirror. Reflected light registers on photographic paper on the drum.

station at different times. By measuring the difference in the times of arrival, an observer can work out how far away the earthquake is. But he will be able to plot its exact position only by comparing his measurements with those of observers in other seismic stations.

The strength of the earthquake can be measured by measuring the strength of the waves. This is given on a scale marked from 0 to 9. The strongest earthquakes have tipped the scale at 8·9.

Because seismic waves travel through the earth, they give us information about the earth's interior. For instance, S waves do not travel through liquid but P waves do. Using this knowledge, we have been able to find out that the earth's outer core is liquid but the inner core is solid.

HOW TO STOP EARTHQUAKES

Earthquakes are very powerful. But scientists think they may have a way of lessening or even preventing earthquakes that occur near the earth's surface. Where two moving sections of rock are stuck across a fault, tremendous pressure builds up. If this pressure can be released little by little, an earthquake may be prevented.

One way of doing this would be to drill deep holes along the fault. Then water would be pumped down one hole. The water would make the rocks smooth and slippery so that they could move easily, but only as far as the holes on either side, which are kept dry. Each hole would be treated with water in turn, so that the rocks along the fault would make small, harmless movements, instead of shaking violently and destructively.

This method may need several years of testing before it can be shown to be successful. Hopefully, it may be ready to go into action before the next major earthquake.

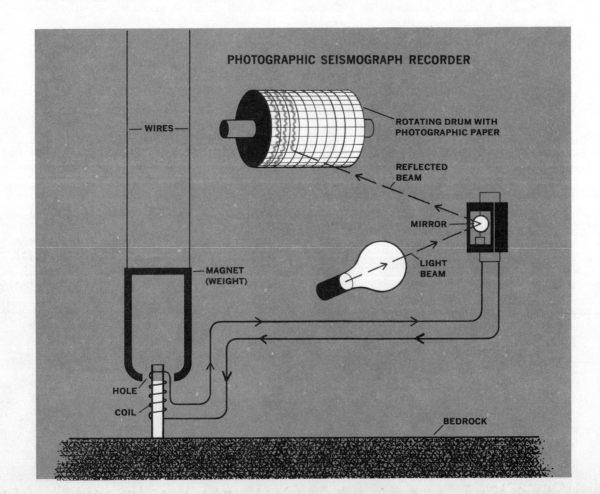

PHOTOGRAPHIC SEISMOGRAPH RECORDER

WIRES

ROTATING DRUM WITH PHOTOGRAPHIC PAPER

REFLECTED BEAM

MIRROR

MAGNET (WEIGHT)

LIGHT BEAM

HOLE

COIL

BEDROCK

Fire From the Earth

Grey, powdery ash drifted down like dirty snow over the city of St. Pierre on the island of Martinique in the West Indies. It crunched beneath the wheels of carriages in the streets. It found its way into houses and into food and drinking water. Every now and then the choking smell of burning sulphur swept through the city. A few birds lay dead on the ground. From time to time, people glanced up uneasily at Mount Pelée, the volcano that rose to a height of 4,000 feet (1,200 meters) just north of the city.

A few people decided to leave, but most stayed on. The volcano had erupted some 50 years earlier, and no one had been hurt.

Then, on the morning of 8 May 1902, just before 7 o'clock, it happened. Some officers on a ship in the harbor were looking at the smoking mountain. Suddenly a great black jet shot out towards them and grew rapidly into a boiling, billowing cloud. In less than a minute, it had swept across the city to the harbor. Everyone in its path was swallowed up by unbearable heat and fumes.

Lava flowing from a volcano can destroy everything in its path.

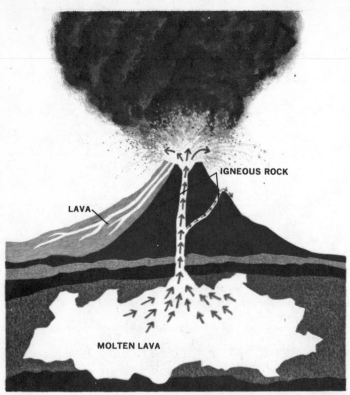

During a volcanic eruption, pressure deep in the earth forces rock and gas to the surface through a vent.

workshop of Vulcan, the blacksmith god. There, Vulcan forged the armor of the gods and the thunderbolts of Jupiter.

A VOLCANO IS BORN

A volcano is the top of a deep crack in the earth's surface. Pressure deep inside the earth forces a mixture of rock and gas up the crack to the surface. The rock is usually hot—in most cases it is so hot that it is molten, or melted. The outburst is called a volcanic *eruption*, and the opening itself is a volcanic *vent*.

The molten rock is known as *magma* before it reaches the surface. After that, it becomes *lava*. Lava contains gases that react rather like the gas in a bottle of fizzy lemonade. If you open the bottle slowly, the gas bubbles slowly out of the lemonade. But if you shake the bottle first, and then open it, the gas rushes out in a great spray, and the lemonade shoots from the bottle.

Some eruptions are gentle. The lava is thin and runny, and the gases bubble out of it easily. The lava pours in rivers of fire from the vent of the volcano, setting trees and bushes and even houses alight. Where the lava is thick and pasty, the gases escape by exploding from the lava, and the eruption is violent.

In another minute or two, the cloud had passed. The air cleared to show the flaming ruins of a once beautiful city. In the harbor, many ships had overturned or were sinking. A few survivors struggled in the water. On shore, all but one of the city's 30,000 people were dead.

THE THREAT OF VOLCANOES

Luckily, disasters such as the one at St. Pierre have been few. But throughout history, people living near volcanoes have felt threatened. Even so, they have continued to live there because the soil produced from volcanic rock is very rich, and people can harvest good crops by farming near volcanoes.

Volcanoes have always terrified and fascinated people. They play a part in many ancient legends. In some, volcanoes are shown as gateways to the underworld. In others, they are the smoking chimneys of the underground

BELTS OF FIRE

At various times in the past, volcanoes have erupted in almost every part of the world. Ancient lava flows have been found in Britain, the eastern United States, Sweden, South Africa, Australia and in many other places where there are no volcanoes today.

Most volcanoes are now found in clearly marked belts, or regions. The main belt encircles the Pacific in a ring of fire. Another belt runs from Indo-

Above: A volcanic eruption off the coast of Iceland in 1963 gave birth to a new island, called Surtsey. Below: Today, most of the active volcanoes occur in clearly marked regions. The main belt is found round the Pacific.

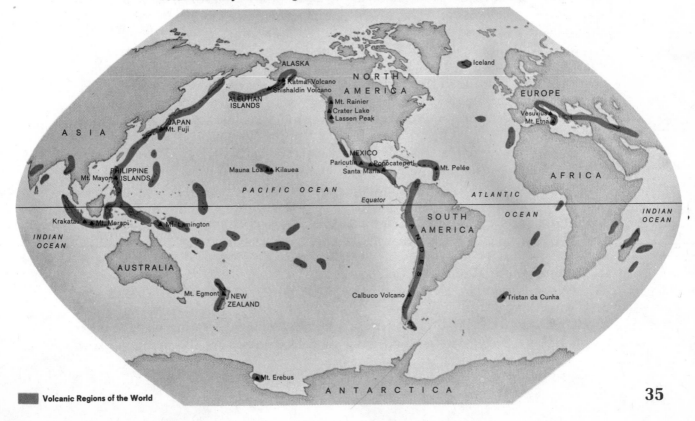

Volcanic Regions of the World

nesia across Asia to the Mediterranean Sea. A third belt runs down to the center of the Atlantic Ocean, where the mid-oceanic islands are all the summits of undersea volcanoes. These belts are in the same position as the earthquake belts, because earthquakes and volcanoes often occur together and for the same reason. Volcanoes rise where the earth's crust is weak and cracked. This happens at the edges of the rocky plates beneath the earth's crust. As the moving plates collide and separate, the movements weaken the surface rocks above their edges.

KINDS OF VOLCANOES

Each volcano erupts in its own way. A *central volcano* is one with a vent opening from a single pipe, and a crater at the top. As lava flows from the vent, it cools and becomes solid, and the volcano builds up. If the lava is thin and runny, it spreads out over a wide area. This produces a broad, low volcano known as a *shield volcano*, because of its shape. The volcanoes in Hawaii, the largest in the world, are shield volcanoes.

If the lava is thick, it does not flow far but builds up in a steep cone round the vent. The cone is made of layers of lava and ash, and the volcano is called a *strato-volcano*. Vesuvius, in Italy, is of this type.

Fissure volcanoes, unlike central volcanoes, build up over many cracks in the earth's crust. Usually the lava is thin and floods out to form large flat plains, or plateaus. This is happening today in Iceland. Such eruptions are called *flood eruptions*.

The eruption of Mount Pelée in 1902 was very unusual. The lava was thick, and when the gas in it exploded, it produced a glowing cloud of hot fragments of lava. This glowing cloud was the first of its kind. Erupting volcanoes are called *active volcanoes*. The eruption usually continues for only a fairly short time, lasting from a few months to about 2 years. The eruption ends when the vent gets plugged with solid lava.

The volcano then quiets down and is said to be *dormant* (sleeping). The crater may fill with water, forming a crater lake. But gas pressure may still be building up below. Sooner or later, the volcano explodes and a new eruption starts. Some volcanoes erupt regularly. Others have never yet been known to erupt. These volcanoes are said to be *extinct* (dead).

TIMELY WARNINGS

There is nothing we can do to stop a volcano from erupting. But scientists keep a close watch on the volcanoes that are most active. They can sometimes tell in advance when an eruption is about to occur. The people nearby can then move out of the area until it is safe to return.

At one time, it was thought that nothing could stop a flow of lava. This meant that, although people and animals could be moved, homes and other buildings were doomed. But in 1973 a way was found to block a lava flow. A harbor in the Westmann Islands off Iceland was threatened by lava. Powerful water pumps were brought in to soak the advancing wall of lava. The water cooled the lava enough to thicken it, and the wall stopped moving. The lava flow changed its course and the harbor was saved.

HOT SPRINGS AND GEYSERS

Rocks near a volcano are warm, and in volcanic regions spring water is often hot. Hot springs are also found in places

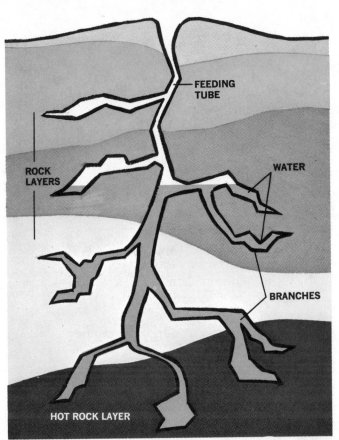

Left: How a geyser looks underground. Hot water is forced up the feeding tube to the opening in the earth. Right: The water and steam from a geyser erupt above the ground like a giant fountain.

where water runs deep underground through heated rock.

Iceland has thousands of hot springs. Hot water is piped from many of them into homes and greenhouses to provide heat. In New Zealand, steam from underground hot springs is used to generate electricity. Because the water is hot, it dissolves minerals in the ground. Some people believe that these warm mineral waters are health-giving. So many towns with hot springs become popular resorts known as spas.

Some kinds of hot springs are called *geysers*, which is an Icelandic name. A geyser regularly spurts hot water and steam into the air from an opening in the ground. It plays like a fountain for

a while and then dies down. After a period of quiet, the geyser suddenly springs into life again. The water may rise many feet into the air. Old Faithful, a geyser in Yellowstone National Park in the United States, sends a column of steaming spray 150 feet (46 meters) into the air. It erupts every 66 minutes.

A geyser is made up of a network of narrow underground passages. They lead down to a layer of hot rocks. When the network of tubes is filling with water, the geyser is quiet. Then the water suddenly boils. A jet of hot water and steam is driven up the passages and bursts from the opening at the top. The geyser then remains quiet for a further period while it is recharged with water.

The Three Great Kinds of Rocks

Wherever you may be, as you read this, you are almost certain to be surrounded by rock. The soil in your garden is made up of tiny grains of rock, and rests on a bed of solid rock. Bricks and concrete are also made from grains of rock. Even if you are reading this on board a ship or by the seaside, rock is still not far away. The water on which you may be sailing covers a huge basin of rock, and the sand on the beach is made up of tiny grains of rock.

Rock comes in all shapes and sizes, from soil and sand, through stones and pebbles to mountains, which are huge pieces of rock. In fact, the earth is a great ball of rock. If we could weigh our planet, it would tip the scales at 6,600,000,000,000,000,000,000 tons.

COLLECT YOUR OWN ROCKS

You will find that collecting rocks can be an interesting hobby, especially if you live near hills or mountains, where many different kinds can be found. Stones and pebbles have many different patterns and colors. You can make them look more attractive by polishing them in a tumbler. This is a little machine that rubs them with a special powder. Some stones and pebbles may be so hard that you may have to polish them for weeks. Others may be so soft that they break up into powder in the tumbler.

As your collection grows, you will want to group, or classify, your finds in some way. You could do this by arranging the stones into groups of different colors, or perhaps into those with bands and those without bands. You could also classify them according to the places where you found the stones.

But a geologist (a scientist who studies the earth) would find that these ways of classifying rocks do not tell him very much about them. He would prefer to group the rocks according to the minerals they contain or the ways in which they form.

THE BIG THREE

Minerals are the chemical substances of which rocks are made. There are many different minerals, and some rocks

Red sandstone: sandstone is a sedimentary rock. It is formed from small grains of rock which change, under great pressure, into hard layers. Sandstone is sometimes used in the construction of buildings.

are mixtures of minerals. You will need many small groups to classify rocks by their minerals. So it is better to classify rocks according to the way they form, because there are only three kinds of rock formations. They are *igneous, sedimentary* and *metamorphic* rocks. Every rock you handle—whether it is a heavy stone, a pebble or a handful of sand or soil—belongs to one of these three groups. Mountains are so large that they may contain more than one group.

Igneous rocks are those that form when hot molten rock rises from the earth's interior, then cools and hardens. *Igneous* is a good name for this kind, because it means 'fiery'. Sedimentary rocks grow from layers of *sediment*— deposits of sand, mud, clay, minerals and even animal or plant remains. The layers build up and slowly harden into rock. Metamorphic rocks form when great heat or pressure underground acts on existing rocks and changes them into new rocks. *Metamorphic* means 'changed'. Although they form underground, these rocks may later come to the surface.

Sedimentary rocks are the most common of these three great classes. They cover two-thirds of the earth's solid surface, including the ocean floors. Most of the remaining rock is igneous, and igneous rock always lies beneath sedimentary rock. It forms the bases of continents and cores of mountains, and supports the sedimentary rock on the ocean floor.

Igneous Rock—Hot and Cold

Round the earth's solid inner core is an outer core of rock which is molten. Other rock inside the earth is hot enough to melt, but the great pressure of cold rock on the surface keeps it solid. Where the pressure is lessened, such as in a passage opening towards the earth's surface, the rock can melt. This molten rock is called *magma*. It rises slowly towards the surface. If it reaches the surface, it spouts from volcanoes in fiery rivers of molten rock that is then called *lava*. Eventually the lava cools and hardens to produce igneous rock. Sometimes the magma does not get as far as the surface but cools and hardens beneath it. The sur-

Marble (below) is a metamorphic rock that is formed from limestone. It has great beauty and strength. The igneous rock basalt (right) was once molten rock. It is often crushed and used to make roads.

face rocks may then gradually weather away to show the mass of igneous rock beneath. Igneous rocks that form at the surface are called *extrusive rocks*, and those that form below are called *intrusive rocks*.

There are many different types of igneous rocks, depending on the minerals in the lava or magma and on how fast it cools and hardens. If the cooling is very rapid, the result is a natural black glass called *obsidian*. The broken edges of obsidian, like those of any glass, are very sharp. American Indians made arrowheads, spear points and knives out of obsidian chips.

Most igneous rocks are made of masses of small grains, or crystals. The crystals form as the molten rock cools and hardens. The slower the cooling, the larger the crystals. Glassy rocks form when the cooling is so rapid that there is no time for crystals to grow. Lava cools more quickly than magma, because it is open to the air at the earth's surface. It usually forms a fine-grained rock called *basalt*. Basalt may be crushed and used in road building. Sometimes basalt produces long columns of rock with several straight, flat sides. The steps of the Giant's Causeway in Northern Ireland are the tops of basalt columns. This outcrop of rock sticks out into the sea towards Scotland. According to legend, it was the beginning of a giant's roadway across the water.

The grains in basalt are so small that they cannot be seen with the unaided eye. Another common igneous rock is *granite*, which has larger grains, or cry-

Left: Cliff made of long columns of basalt. Below: Magma, or molten rock, slowly rises towards the earth's surface. The magma may cool before it reaches the surface, forming a rock called granite.

INTRUSION

MAGMA HARDENS INTO GRANITE

MAGMA

stals. This is because granite is an intrusive rock. It forms when magma cools underground. Being underground, away from the cold air, magma cools slowly thus allowing large crystals to grow. Granite and basalt are made up of several different minerals. Each mineral forms separate crystals as the liquid rock cools. In granite, those crystals are often large enough to be seen. They make up grainy patterns of pink and grey in the rock.

Whole mountains of granite, once the cores of much bigger mountains, lie exposed at the earth's surface. Parts of the Highlands of Scotland are made of granite. The rock is very hard, and when polished, the grains produce a beautiful shine. Granite is often used for making roads and in large public buildings.

Much lava contains bubbles of gas. When the lava cools, it hardens into a kind of solid froth called *pumice*. The bubbles, which are trapped inside, make the pumice so light that it floats on water. Pumice is often ground into fine powder and used as a polisher.

Shaping Sedimentary Rocks

Everything in our world is continually being broken down. Rocks are worn away by wind and ice, minerals are turned into liquid by water, and all living things die. But our world is also ever-changing, and these materials and remains are not lost, but are used again to form sedimentary rocks.

Grains of rocks produced by the *erosion* (wearing away) of rock masses eventually settle in layers on the beds of seas, lakes and rivers. As these layers get thicker and heavier, the lower ones are pressed down. They may also be squeezed by rock movements; and minerals left in them by water may cement the grains together. In these

Limestone (above) is made from the shells of millions of tiny sea creatures. Granite (below) is made up of different minerals which form separate crystals.

41

ways, over a period of hundreds of thousands of years, the sediments become layers of hard rock.

Sandstone is one example of this kind of sedimentary rock. The layers that make it up can often be seen in sandstone cliffs. Sandstone may be strong enough to be used as building stone. Shale is a similar sedimentary rock formed from tiny bits of mud and clay. The rock can easily be split into its layers, and is crushed to make tiles, bricks and cement. Shale is the most common sedimentary rock.

Certain minerals can be dissolved by water. This happens when water flows over rocks containing those minerals. That is how the sea became salty. In some places, water containing a mineral in its dissolved state may be trapped in a pool. If the water evaporates (changes into vapor or gas) with the heat of the sun, the mineral is left as a layer on the ground where the pool was. A rock slowly builds up if this occurs many times. Rock salt is one kind of sedimentary rock that forms in this way.

Limestone is a well-known sedimentary rock that forms from the remains of animals. It begins as tiny shells of dead sea animals settle in layers on the ocean floor. Gradually it hardens into rock. Some of the shells are large enough for their remains to be seen in pieces of limestone. Lime—a substance used in glass, and in mortar for joining bricks and stones—is produced from limestone.

Coal is sedimentary rock. It comes from peat, which is formed from layers of dead plants. Sometimes the outline of a leaf can be seen in a piece of coal. In fact, fossils (preserved remains) can be found only in sedimentary rocks. In other rocks, the heat that made them destroys any remains of plants and ani-mals. Sedimentary rocks, therefore, are like books in which scientists can read the story of life on earth.

Metamorphic Rocks: All Change

There are always movements going on all over the earth's surface and inside it. These movements sometimes put a great strain on the rocks. Masses of hot igneous rock may rise towards the surface and heat other rocks in their path. Great movements may squeeze, fold and twist the rocks. Because of this, rocks change. Sedimentary and igneous rocks become metamorphic rocks, and existing metamorphic rocks may change to new metamorphic rocks. Shale becomes slate; the thin layers of soft shale change into the hard layers of slate that are sometimes used for making roofs. Limestone becomes marble, another metamorphic rock.

Pure marble is white, but small amounts of other minerals and rocks may streak it with light brown or pink. Marble is sometimes used to make buildings look more beautiful, and many of the world's finest statues are made of white marble. Quartzite is a metamorphic rock formed from sandstone. The sand grains in the sandstone join together, producing a very hard rock. *Schist* and *gneiss* are general names for two kinds of metamorphic rocks. A schist is made up of thin layers of minerals, and a gneiss contains light and dark bands.

When you look at rocks, remember that new rocks like them are being formed all the time. The rocks you see will eventually be destroyed, and from their remains new rocks will be formed. Rocks are hard and last for a long time—but even they are part of nature's ever-changing pattern.

Floating Mountains of Ice

In April 1912, the largest ship that had ever been built began its first voyage from England to the United States. Named the *Titanic*, the liner was said to be unsinkable. But the claim was to be very short-lived. On the night of 14 April, off the Grand Banks south of Newfoundland, the *Titanic* hit an iceberg and sank, killing about 1,500 people.

Icebergs are like mountains of fresh-water ice floating in the sea. Some of them are so big that they look like snow-covered islands. Icebergs float because ice is a little lighter than water. But they float low in the water. The part that we can see above the waves is only one-tenth to one-eighth of the whole iceberg. The rest lies hidden beneath the water. Great spurs of ice may stick out under the surface, so that it is very dangerous for ships to sail anywhere near icebergs.

HOW ICEBERGS ARE BORN

Icebergs are pieces of ice that break off the ice-sheets that cover the land in polar regions. Most icebergs in the Northern Hemisphere come from Greenland. In the Southern Hemisphere, the icebergs are formed in Antarctica. At the edges of the ice-sheets, great glaciers (rivers of ice) slide slowly down to the sea. As they move into the water, the ends of the glaciers break off and form icebergs. This way in which icebergs form is called *calving*.

Icebergs in the North Atlantic flow southwards. Arrows show the direction of flow.

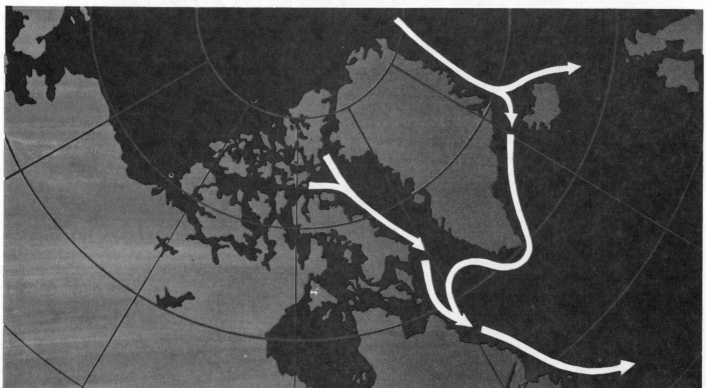

The main part of an iceberg lies under the water.

For hours before calving actually takes place, a low, rumbling sound can sometimes be heard. Then a loud cracking noise fills the air as the iceberg breaks away. People close enough can hear the hiss of escaping air as bubbles that were trapped in the ice burst open.

Glaciers calve all the year round. But more icebergs drift away to the open sea in summer. During the winter, the icebergs are hemmed in near the land by frozen sea water. In spring, the pack-ice (a mass of large pieces of ice driven together by wind and currents) around the shore melts. Whole fleets of icebergs are carried by currents out to the ocean.

Icebergs are a wonderful sight. They are shining white or light blue in colour. In northern seas, the icebergs often appear in strange, jagged shapes. They may look like ghostly floating castles with spires and turrets, gleaming white against the sky. In southern seas, near Antarctica, icebergs have less exciting shapes—they look like gigantic flat slabs lying in the water. But their size is astonishing. They are usually about half a mile wide and 1 to 10 miles long (1 kilometre wide and 2 to 16 kilometres long). And they are about 900 feet (270 metres) deep on average. The largest iceberg ever seen was 60 miles (96 kilometres) wide and 208 miles (332 kilometres) long—slightly larger than Belgium!

THE LIFE OF AN ICEBERG

Icebergs drift with the ocean currents. In the North Atlantic, they are carried south by the cold currents that flow southwards past Greenland from the Arctic. Off Newfoundland, they are caught by the Gulf Stream, a warm current that flows up from the Gulf of Mexico. Then the icebergs may be carried into the shipping lanes. As a result, ships sailing in the Atlantic take more southerly routes in the spring and summer in order to avoid icebergs.

An iceberg starts to break up as soon as it is afloat. Cracks open up on the surface, and during the day they may fill with water from melting snow and ice. At night, the water may freeze. As it does so, it takes up more room and widens the cracks. The iceberg is weakened, and pieces start to fall off and float away. Gradually the iceberg becomes smaller and smaller. If it enters a warm current, it usually melts completely within a few days.

Southern icebergs have a longer life than northern icebergs. Not only are they bigger, and because of this take longer to break up and melt, but the currents of the southern seas keep them in cold water. They may float there for many years before they disappear.

THE DANGEROUS ICEBERGS

Large icebergs may float a long way before they break up or melt. Ships try to keep clear of them, but they are impossible to see at night or in fog. Even radar, which can pierce the dark and the fog with radio pulses, cannot show low icebergs that lurk just above the surface of the sea. Where cold and warm ocean currents meet, fog often occurs. The cold currents also bring icebergs. So these places, such as the Grand Banks of Newfoundland, are very dangerous to shipping.

After the *Titanic* sank near Newfoundland, many nations met to talk about ways of making sure that such a terrible thing would never happen again. The following year, the International Ice Patrol was set up. Two years after the sinking of the *Titantic*, it began to keep track of icebergs in the North Atlantic and to mark their positions on a map. The patrol is manned by the United States Coast Guard. Countries whose ships use the North Atlantic, help to pay for the cost of the patrol.

The International Ice Patrol keeps a watch on the North Atlantic by aircraft

An iceberg off the coast of Greenland. Atlantic icebergs look like jagged crystal mountains.

and ship. It normally works from February to July. During the rest of the year, the freezing of the polar seas traps the icebergs in the far north. Twice a day during the spring and summer, the patrol sends radio messages to ships in the North Atlantic shipping lanes. It reports the position, size and likely course of any iceberg in the neighbourhood.

WATERING THE DESERTS

Antarctic icebergs are not nearly so dangerous to shipping. They are very large and therefore easily seen. They are not usually found in shipping lanes, but their sides are smooth, so that ships can safely pass by quite near to them. Some scientists are now saying that these icebergs could provide the peoples of the world with new sources of fresh water.

The plan would be to lassoo Antarctic icebergs with cables and join them up in 'trains'. A powerful ship would then act as 'locomotive', and pull the train of icebergs to the dry coasts of California, Chile, Australia, or anywhere else in need of fresh water. The journey would be very slow—it would take nearly a year to get from the Antarctic to, say, California. As the icebergs passed through the water, much of the ice would melt. So the icebergs would have to be wrapped in plastic sheeting to protect them. As soon as they arrived at the end of their journey, the icebergs would be towed close to land and broken into small chunks that could be piped ashore.

Fresh water from icebergs might be much cheaper in dry areas than fresh water obtained in any other way. How much such a scheme would cost is now being worked out. If it is not too much, men could soon be mining Antarctic ice.

Oceans of the World

We call our planet 'earth', but this is not really the best name for it. If you take a globe and turn it so that the centre of the Pacific Ocean faces you, you will see hardly any land at all. The globe looks as if it is covered with water. Of course it is not. But oceans and seas do cover 70 per cent of the earth's surface. So perhaps a better name for our planet would be 'ocean'. Such a name would also distinguish it more from the other planets of the solar system, none of which has oceans.

THE GREAT BODIES OF WATER

There are many different kinds of bodies of water. Puddles, pools and ponds are bodies of water, as are lakes. These are among the smaller bodies, and normally contain fresh water. The earth's larger bodies of water—bays, gulfs, seas and oceans—almost always contain salt water.

Oceans are the largest bodies of water, and there are only four, or perhaps five, of them. Seas are much smaller and are usually located at the edges of oceans, where parts of the ocean are almost surrounded by land. In fact, seas are arms of the larger oceans. Sometimes the smaller seas are called gulfs or bays. A few seas are completely inland and are not linked with any ocean. These are really huge lakes.

There are only five **bodies** of water that are so large that they **can** be called oceans: the Pacific Ocean, the Atlantic Ocean, the Indian Ocean, the Arctic Ocean and, according to some geographers, the Antarctic Ocean.

The Mighty Pacific

The world's largest ocean is the Pacific Ocean. It covers 64,000,000 square miles (165,760,000 square kilometres), almost a third of the globe. The Pacific is larger than all the land on the earth put together! East to west, the Pacific stretches for 10,500 miles (16,898 kilometres)—nearly halfway round the world. From north to south, it extends from the Bering Strait to 60° south latitude—a distance of about 8,400 miles (13,518 kilometres).

The coastlines of North and South America form the eastern boundary of the Pacific. The western boundary is more difficult to define because there are many large islands separated from the Asiatic and Australian mainland by shallow seas. This mighty ocean also contains the deepest point on earth: Challenger Deep, a part of the Marianas Trench near Guam, in the western Pacific. The bottom lies 36,198 feet (11,033 metres) below the surface.

The Wide Open Atlantic Ocean

The Atlantic Ocean is the second largest ocean. Its area is 31,830,000 square miles (82,439,700 square kilometres)—half the size of the Pacific Ocean. Its deepest point is the Milwaukee Depth near Puerto Rico, where the ocean bed is 30,246 feet (9,219 metres) below the surface.

Most of the bottom of the Atlantic Ocean is covered with mud made up of the shells of tiny ocean animals. The ocean bed is divided into two valleys by the mid-Atlantic ridge. This is an S-shaped ridge running from north to south and rising about 6,000 feet (1,829 metres) from the ocean bottom. The ridge rises above sea level in many places, appearing as the islands of the Azores, St Paul Rocks, Ascension, St Helena, Tristan da Cunha and Bouvet.

The North Atlantic has a very uneven shoreline compared with the fairly straight coast of the South Atlantic. The largest bays or seas are formed by the Baltic, the North Sea, the Mediterranean and the Black Sea.

The Baltic Sea in northern Europe is bordered by Denmark, Sweden, Finland, Poland, Germany and the Soviet Union. Much of the Baltic is frozen for 3 to 5 months each year, so ships can only sail those waters during the ice-free months.

The North Sea lies between Great Britain and the European continent. More than half the world's herring supply comes from the North Sea. The warming influence of the Gulf Stream, which flows into the north of the North Sea, keeps the main ports free from ice in winter. These ports include Rotterdam, London, Antwerp, Bremen and Hamburg.

The Mediterranean Sea has been perhaps the most important sea in the history of Western man. The name means 'in the midst of lands', and indeed it is nearly landlocked between Europe, Asia and Africa. In the west, the narrow

OCEAN DEPTHS OF THE WORLD

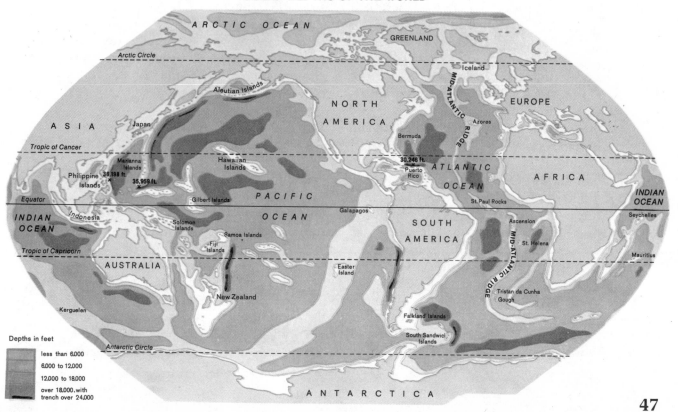

Depths in feet

less than 6,000
6,000 to 12,000
12,000 to 18,000
over 18,000, with trench over 24,000

Strait of Gibraltar connects it with the Atlantic Ocean. Its eastern outlet, to the Red Sea, is by way of the Suez Canal. Most of the people who live along the shores of the Mediterranean earn a living by farming. There is an important export trade in citrus fruits, tobacco, olive and other vegetable oils, cotton, wine and winter wheat. Mines are worked throughout the Mediterranean region.

Leading off from the Mediterranean, through a series of straits at its north-eastern corner, is the Black Sea. It lies between Europe and Asia. The sea is almost ice-free all the year round. Its principal ports are Odessa and Sevastopol (Soviet Union), Varna (Bulgaria), Constanta (Romania) and Trabzon (Turkey).

The coastal waters on the American side of the Atlantic include Hudson Bay, the Gulf of St Lawrence, the Gulf of Mexico and the Caribbean Sea.

The Caribbean lies between the southern coast of the United States and the northern coast of South America. It contains several hundred islands, most of which belong to the Greater or Lesser Antilles. These islands stretch for some 2,000 miles (3,220 kilometres) from Florida to Venezuela. The four largest islands are Cuba, Hispaniola (Haiti and the Dominican Republic), Jamaica and Puerto Rico.

The Indian Ocean

The Indian Ocean is the third largest ocean. It has an area of 28,350,000 square miles (73,426,500 square kilometres). Its greatest depth, the Diamantina Deep, is 26,400 feet (8,047 metres). The ocean is surrounded by land on three sides but open to the south. In the north-west is the Arabian Sea, between India and Arabia, and the long, narrow Red Sea, between Arabia and Africa.

Some important rivers empty into the Indian Ocean—the Indus, Ganges, Irrawaddy, Brahmaputra and Shatt al Arab from Asia, and the Zambesi and Limpopo from Africa. There are two very large islands in the Indian Ocean—Madagascar off the south-eastern coast of Africa, and Sri Lanka off the southern tip of India. Apart from these, a number of smaller islands and groups of islands are scattered throughout the ocean.

The Frozen Arctic

The smallest ocean is the Arctic Ocean. It has an area of 5,440,000 square miles (14,089,600 square kilometres), and is 17,850 feet (5,441 metres) at its deepest point. The ocean is almost surrounded by the northern shores of North America, Europe and Asia, and is largely covered by floating ice. The water has little salt because many rivers empty into the Arctic Ocean. Only a small amount of water is turned into water vapour because of the intense cold.

Many Canadian and Siberian islands lie in the shallow seas fringing the deep Arctic basin. Several major rivers flow into it, among them the Yenisei, Ob, Lena and Mackenzie.

The Antarctic: An Ocean for Some

Some people say that the world has a fifth ocean—the Antarctic Ocean—surrounding the continent of Antarctica. But others say that this is only the southern parts of the Pacific, Atlantic and Indian oceans, and that it has no marked boundaries. It is a cold ocean, swept by the roaring forties (stormy west winds) blowing round Antarctica. The seas off Cape Horn at the southern tip of South America are usually very stormy. Most ships travel between the Atlantic and Pacific through the Panama

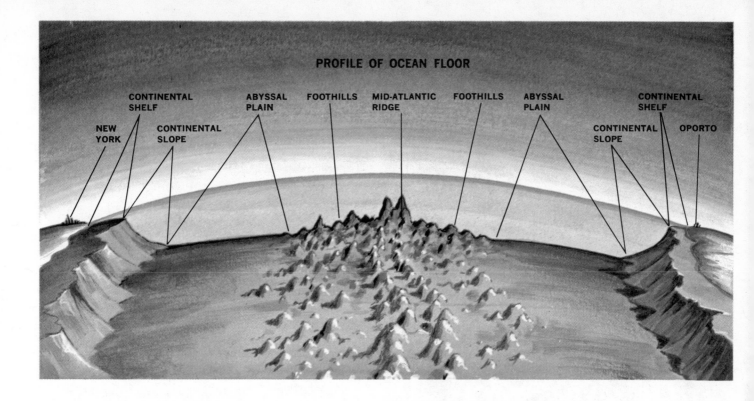

NEW YORK

CONTINENTAL SHELF

CONTINENTAL SLOPE

ABYSSAL PLAIN

FOOTHILLS

MID-ATLANTIC RIDGE

FOOTHILLS

ABYSSAL PLAIN

CONTINENTAL SLOPE

CONTINENTAL SHELF

OPORTO

Canal, north of the Equator, rather than make a long journey southwards into dangerous waters.

The Antarctic Ocean may discourage human beings but it is rich in animal life. Seals and whales abound; and penguins spend much of their time in its waters. The sea animals and birds feed on fish, small shrimps and plankton (tiny floating plants and animals).

BENEATH THE WAVES

Imagine you have a special kind of submarine that can take you to any part of any ocean. What would you see and what would you find out about the ocean as you travelled through it?

As you leave the shore, you can see the sea floor gently sloping downwards beneath you. As you plunge deeper, the light becomes a darker blue. When you are 300 feet (90 meters) down, there is only a little light left. Your ship must have its own lights so that you can see where you are going. The sea floor goes down to a depth of about 600 feet (180 meters) and then levels out. This part of

the sea floor is called the *continental shelf*. A shelf surrounds all the continents, jutting out below the sea as far as 300 miles (500 kilometers) from the shore.

Suddenly, the shelf comes to an end. The sea floor falls sharply away. This steep slope is called the *continental slope*. It sweeps down without a break to the bottom of the ocean.

Here and there, deep canyons cut back into the continental slope. Sometimes these canyons lead back to valleys on the continental shelf, and may even link up with rivers on the land. But usually the canyon starts near the edge of the shelf.

A Flat Plain of Mud

We are now sailing over a deep plain, some 3 miles (5 kilometers) below the surface of the ocean. The bottom is very flat, because it is built up of layers of mud and other sediment. This is picked up by the seawater as it rushes down the continental slope, and then dropped as the water slows down on reaching the flat ocean floor. This part

49

abyssal plain. Only a few of these mountains are high enough to form islands.

Deep Splits in the Plain

Underwater trenches sometimes form great gashes in the abyssal plain. They may go down as far below the plain as the abyssal plain is below the surface of the ocean. The trenches are long and narrow, with cliff-like walls on both sides. They are found at the edges of the coasts or alongside chains of islands. In Chile, the continental shelf is very narrow. The land falls quickly from the tops of the Andes Mountains to the depths of an offshore trench—from 20,000 feet (6,000 metres) above sea level to 24,000 feet (7,200 metres) below it. This is the greatest slope on earth, falling 44,000 feet in 250 miles (13,200 metres in 400 kilometres).

The formation of ocean mountains and trenches is connected with the drifting of the continents. Continental drift tells us how the oceans came to be formed. You can read about this in 'The Ever-Changing Earth'. (See page 21.)

FRESH AND SALT WATER

Only 3 per cent of our water is fresh water. The remaining 97 per cent is the salt water of the oceans and seas. But, although we cannot drink it, we must have the water of the oceans in order to keep our supply of fresh water.

Fresh water comes from the rain that falls from the clouds in the sky. The raindrops are formed from water vapor in the air. This water vapor comes from water in the oceans and seas, and in rivers and lakes. It also comes from animals and plants. The salt from sea-water and other salt water gets left behind when water vapor forms. That is why rain water is always fresh.

of the ocean is called the *abyss*, and the sea floor is known as the *abyssal plain*. The abyss may continue until we reach the other side of the ocean. There the floor abruptly rises up to form a continental slope, then a shelf surrounding the land on the other side.

But here and there, we may first come to great underground mountains, or *sea mounts*. These mountains are usually formed by volcanoes, and their tops may poke above the waves as islands.

Underneath the world's oceans runs a great long ridge of undersea mountains. Their height is normally about 6,000 feet (2,000 meters) above the

How Water Helps Us

Some water vapor that forms over the oceans is blown by winds over the land. There it joins water vapor that comes from the land. Rain falls and feeds rivers that flow to the sea. We use the water on its journey to the sea, taking it from rivers or lakes, or storing it in reservoirs. We need the water for drinking and washing, and we also use it to make electricity.

A lot of water flows into the oceans from rivers, and even more falls as rain into the sea. But the oceans and seas do not overflow, because the amount of water that enters the ocean is equal to the amount lost by being turned into water vapor. This movement of water from sea and land to the air and back again is called the water cycle.

SEAWATER AND ITS SALT

Seawater tastes salty because rivers carry with them some salts from the rocks on land, and these salts then collect in the oceans. The main salt is sodium chloride—common table salt. People often take this salt from the sea by collecting seawater in large, shallow pans on the shore, and allowing the water to be turned into vapor by the heat of the sun. The salt is left behind, coating the sides and bottoms of the pans.

Seawater also contains many other substances made up of most of the elements. Some of these are there in amounts large enough to make it worthwhile removing them. Magnesium and bromine are both taken from seawater by various chemical and electrical means.

There are also large amounts of precious metals, such as gold and silver, in the salts of the world's oceans—far more than there are on land. But these amounts are spread out so thinly through the oceans that it would cost far more than they are worth to take them from seawater. On the ocean floor are large deposits of manganese compounds. It may one day be worth mining these deposits for use in making steel.

In the depths of the abyss and in polar regions, the water may be at freezing-point or even below it. Yet the water

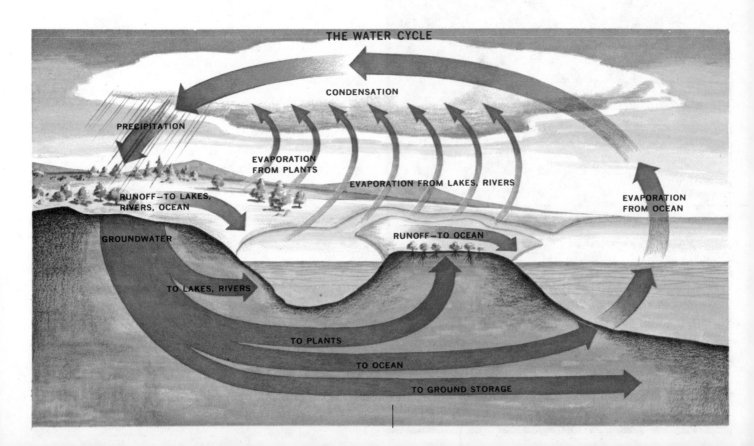

THE WATER CYCLE

CONDENSATION

PRECIPITATION

EVAPORATION FROM PLANTS

EVAPORATION FROM LAKES, RIVERS

EVAPORATION FROM OCEAN

RUNOFF—TO LAKES, RIVERS, OCEAN

RUNOFF—TO OCEAN

GROUNDWATER

TO LAKES, RIVERS

TO PLANTS

TO OCEAN

TO GROUND STORAGE

still does not turn to ice, because the salt in the water lowers its freezing-point. That is why salt is spread on snow and ice in winter to make it melt. You can often see ice and snow covering the shore when the sea is still free of ice. But if it is very cold indeed, the sea will eventually ice over at the shore. In polar regions, ice will form in mid-ocean as well.

We cannot drink seawater and live, because our body fluids have much less salt in them than seawater. If we take in extra salt, we upset the delicate balance of chemicals in our bodies. Some animals can live in the sea because their body fluids have the same level of salt as seawater.

THE LIVING SEA

All animal life on earth depends on plant life. In the sea, floating at and near the surface, are great pastures of plant life.

Photograph of plankton, magnified many times. These tiny plants and animals live in the ocean.

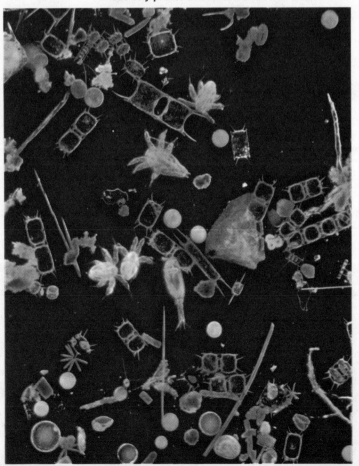

Instead of grass, the pastures are made up of tiny plants that float in the water. They live there because they need sunlight to grow, just like land plants. They also need minerals, which they get from the remains of dead sea plants and animals.

Pastures of Plenty

The tiny plants, together with equally small drifting animals, make up one of the great classes of sea life. This class is called *plankton*. The tiny animals in the plankton feed on the plants there. The living things that make up the plankton are so small that a bucketful of seawater can hold a million of them. The smallest are single living cells. Seen through a microscope, they may have beautiful and complicated bodies.

The Free Swimmers

Animals that can swim freely in the oceans make up another great class of ocean life. They are known as *nekton*. Many kinds of nekton animals live at the surface, feeding on plankton and on other nekton animals there. Nekton includes all kinds of fishes, birds such as seagulls, reptiles such as turtles, and mammals such as seals and whales. Some of these, including several large whales, feed only on plankton.

Dwellers of the Deep

The third class of ocean life is *benthos* —the plants and animals that live on the sea floor. Plants such as seaweeds grow on the bottom of the continental shelf, where some light from the sun filters through the water. Flatfish hide themselves in the mud or sand, and all kinds of animals live among the rocks.

In the abyss it is completely dark and no plants can grow. Yet strange animals live there. They make their own light and shine with it. Their jaws are large so that they can swallow any of the few animals that come their way, large or small. Some of the deep-sea animals are scavengers—they feed on the remains of plants and animals that drift down from above. The others eat these scavengers, or eat each other.

The In-Betweens

A large number of nekton animals swim in the middle layers of the ocean. The light is too faint for any plant life, so these animals live like the benthos of the abyss—that is, by scavenging or eating each other. They include great shoals of fish, squids and whales.

Using instruments, scientists have also discovered a layer of animal life known as the *deep scattering layer*. During the day, the layer remains deep down where it is dark. At night it rises to the surface, and sinks back when dawn comes. Trawl nets have not yet been able to catch any of the animals in this layer, so this means that they are probably very small and are very fast swimmers. By moving up and down and staying out of the light, they cannot be seen by larger animals that would eat them.

SCIENCE LOOKS AT THE SEA

Oceanography—the study of the sea— is a young science. Man can find out little about the sea without the help of instruments and special ships. The first book on oceanography, *Physical Geography of the Sea* by Matthew Maury, an American naval officer, was published in 1855. The first oceanographic voyage was made by the British naval vessel HMS *Challenger*. It sailed round the world, from 1872 to 1876, taking measurements and collecting specimens.

LIFE IN SHALLOW COASTAL WATERS

JELLYFISH

SPONGE

ELKHORN CORAL

ANEMONE

SEA CUCUMBER

SEA FAN CORAL

SPONGE

CRAB

STAR CORAL

SEA URCHIN

STARFISH

SCALLOPS

SEA URCHIN SHELL

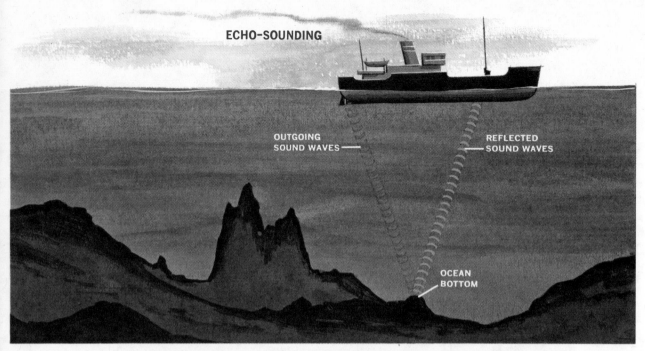

ECHO-SOUNDING

OUTGOING SOUND WAVES —

REFLECTED — SOUND WAVES

OCEAN BOTTOM

Above: This diagram shows how echo-sounding works: sound waves sent from a ship are reflected from the ocean bottom. Below left: A scientist records the ocean depths received from the echo-sounder. Below right: Section of a tracing of the ocean floor.

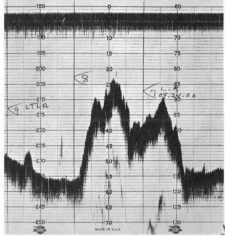

A Tip from World War II

Oceanography then developed slowly until reliable methods of studying the sea were found. Modern oceanography dates only from World War II. In order to find enemy submarines, engineers developed a system called *echo-sounding*. Ships were fitted with special equipment. A transmitter ship sent a pulse of sound through the water, and a receiver picked up any echoes of the sound that came back. If a submarine happened to be in the area, the sound echoed back from it, and was heard in the receiver. The operator noted how long it took for the echo to be picked up by the receiver. Knowing the speed of sound through water, he quickly worked out how far the submarine was from the ship.

Echo-sounding can be used to chart the sea floor and to find shoals of fish. The deep scattering layer was found by echo-sounding. Echo-sounders now automatically draw the shape of the sea floor on a length of paper on which the depth is marked.

Drilling for Samples

Oceanographers also use special automatic instruments to measure ocean currents and temperatures. Samples of seawater are taken by lowering special bottles to certain depths.

In recent years, there has been much interest in drilling samples of mud and other material deposited on the ocean floor. The research ship *Glomar Challenger* can lower a drill to depths of 25,000 feet (7,500 meters). The ship stays in position above the hole being drilled by lowering an acoustic (sound) beacon to the sea floor. The beacon gives off sound signals like an echo-sounder. The ship receives these signals and automatically stays in position above the beacon. The material drilled from the ocean floor has played a major part in helping to confirm scientists' ideas about the earth's formation and movements.

LIVING UNDERWATER

Instruments alone cannot tell us all that we need to know about the oceans. We must also visit them. We now have a few special submarines that allow oceanographers to study life and conditions beneath the waves. They have viewing rooms that allow scientists to see out into the ocean, as well as grabs for collecting specimens. To go deep down, where the water pressure is so great that it would easily crush an ordinary submarine, very strong vessels are needed. These are called *bathyscaphs*. Men in the bathyscaph *Trieste* made a record dive to the bottom of Challenger Deep in 1960.

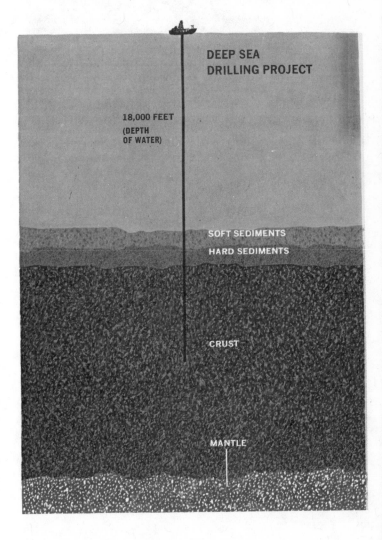

DEEP SEA DRILLING PROJECT

18,000 FEET (DEPTH OF WATER)

SOFT SEDIMENTS

HARD SEDIMENTS

CRUST

MANTLE

An artist's drawing of the United States Navy's underwater experimental station, 'Sealab III'. Aquanauts, such as those shown here, performed tasks both inside and outside their underwater living quarters and research laboratory.

Dangers of the Deep

Even more can be found out about the ocean if men can swim freely beneath the surface. Aqualung and scuba equipment supplies divers with air and so allows them to breathe underwater and swim easily. But there is a limit to the depth they can reach. At about 300 feet (90 meters), the nitrogen in the air being breathed in begins to dissolve in a person's blood. Too much nitrogen in the blood causes a kind of drunkenness, so that the diver does not know what he is doing. If he comes up from a great depth too quickly, the nitrogen bubbles out of his blood, causing great pain and possibly death. To breathe only oxygen at this depth can also be dangerous. But scientists have discovered that if oxygen is mixed with another gas, such as helium or hydrogen, men can dive much deeper. It has allowed one diver to reach a depth of 1,000 feet (305 meters).

Deeper and Deeper

Aquanauts, as these brave divers are called, have lived in undersea stations for up to 2 months at a time. They leave their stations in diving gear and work in the surrounding sea. The stations cannot be too deep, and the divers cannot swim very far up or down, but they are learning a lot about the waters of the continental shelf. The divers talk to others on the surface by telephone, but talking is not easy if they are breathing helium-oxygen mixtures. Helium is so light that it makes the divers' voices sound high and squeaky.

Deep-sea living quarters are now being tested, in which oceanographers could live on the abyssal plain. They would not be able to leave the base to swim freely at such a depth. But they could carry out much useful work at viewing windows, and in tiny submarines that could move away from the main station.

Above: An aquanaut from 'Tektite II', an underwater station, enters a capsule which will take him to a decompression chamber on the surface. Below: A woman aquanaut takes photographs underwater. The mesh bag is used to carry samples of underwater life back to the underwater station.

Ocean Tides and Currents

If you go to a beach on the shore of one of the world's oceans, you will notice that the sea moves. Waves crash on the shore, and boats bob up and down in the sea. If you take a long swim or a boat trip, you will return to find that the edge of the sea has moved up or down the beach. You might have to walk a long way back if the water has gone out. If the water has come in, you might find your clothes floating out to sea. This kind of ocean movement is called a tide. And while you were swimming or boating, you may have noticed that the sea was moving along and carrying you in one direction. This is because of the currents that flow in the sea.

THE WILD WAVES

Waves move towards the shore and tumble over in a splash of foam as they break on the beach. On a windy day, the waves are high and the whole ocean seems to be attacking the land. But the water does not in fact move. When a wave passes, the water level goes up as the crest (highest part) goes by and then down as the trough (lowest part) of the wave passes. The particles of water move in circles, up and down and to and fro. This is why boats bob up and down on the surface of the sea. The waves are caused by winds, and on a calm day there are hardly any waves at all.

At the shore, where the water is very shallow, the wind blows the crest of the wave over and it breaks on the shore. In high winds, the waves may break very violently on the shore. Foaming crests also form out at sea when it is windy, and are often called 'white horses'.

THE RESTLESS TIDES

Suppose you arrive on the beach at 10 o'clock in the morning. A sign tells you that this is the time of high tide, or high water. You can tell by looking at the beach, perhaps by the amount of litter there, that the sand you can see is never washed by the sea.

Soon you will notice that the edge of the water is drawing back, leaving a line of seaweed and a few sticks, shells and bits of rubbish at high-water mark. If the beach is shallow, the water will draw back quickly as it falls. Eventually it stops drawing back, and the ocean is at low tide, or low water. If you check the time, it should be 4:13 in the afternoon, and the tide sign should confirm that this is the time of low tide. The water then begins to come back in again.

If you stay on the beach after dark, you will be there for another high tide—at about 10:25 at night. And if you are there all night, you will see another low tide at 4:38 the following morning. But you are more likely to see the following high tide—at 10:50 the next morning.

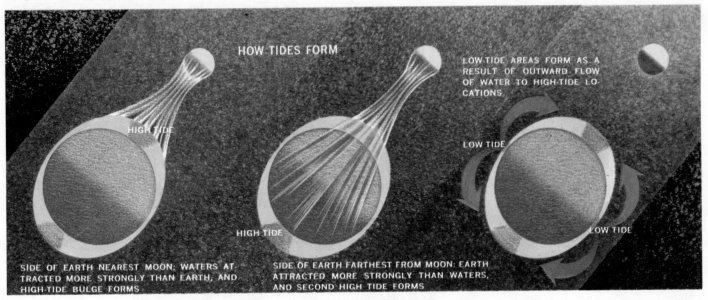

Tides are caused mainly by the moon's gravitational pull on the earth and its waters. For example, on the side of the earth nearest the moon, the waters are attracted more strongly than the earth, so a bulge of water—the high tide—forms.

that a low tide occurs exactly halfway between two high tides and that a high tide happens exactly halfway between two low tides. You will be able to work out that there are 12 hours 25 minutes between two high tides or two low tides. The time for two complete tides to pass is 24 hours 50 minutes, so that the tides get later by 50 minutes each day.

What Makes the Tides?

Tides obviously occur because the water level of the ocean is going up and down twice a day. But why should the level change in this way? Early astronomers discovered that the period of two complete tides—24 hours 50 minutes—is the same as the time from one moonrise to the next. They believed, correctly, that the moon influences the tides. Great forces are at work to raise and lower the oceans. These forces—gravity and centrifugal force—are the same as those that hold together our solar system.

When one heavenly body goes round another, as the moon goes round the earth, both bodies move. They both spin round their center of gravity. This is a point somewhere between the centers of the two bodies, and its position depends on how big they are. (In the case of the earth and moon, the center of gravity is inside the earth.) As they spin round, a force pulls the bodies away from each other. We call this centrifugal force. But the force of gravity that exists between the two bodies pulls them together. Gravity and centrifugal force balance each other, and the smaller body goes round the larger one.

This means that all parts of both bodies —in this case, the earth and moon—are affected by two forces pulling in opposite directions. But, on the side of the earth that faces the moon, the moon's pull of gravity is slightly stronger than the centrifugal force. On the opposite side, the moon is further away and its pull is weaker, and does not equal the pull of the earth's centrifugal force. We do not notice this slight difference in forces, but it is strong enough to affect the water in the oceans. It makes water move towards the side of the earth that faces the moon and also towards the opposite side, raising the ocean levels in these regions. In between these two regions, the level is lowered.

The earth spins round once every 24 hours, but the high-water levels remain facing the moon and opposite it. Therefore, twice a day, one particular point on the earth will come to a high level and have a high tide. In between it gets to a low level and there a low tide will occur. Two complete tides—two high tides and two low tides—take 24 hours 50 minutes. This is because the moon moves an extra 13 degrees on its journey round the earth. The earth has to rotate another 13 degrees before the first high-water point comes back into line with the moon. This takes 50 minutes.

How the Sun Affects the Tides

The earth goes round the sun just as the moon goes round the earth, and the sun raises tides in the same way as the moon does. The sun's influence is less than that of the moon, but it is strong enough to show in the tides. When the sun, earth and moon are in line, the sun and moon act together for their greatest pull on the tide. The *tidal range* (the difference in height between high tide and low tide) increases and there are very high tides and very low tides. This happens every fortnight at full moon and new moon, and such tides are called the *spring tides*. (The name has nothing to do with the spring of the year.) Between these times, the sun and moon are at right angles to the earth. They are pulling against each other, so that their effect on the tides is at its lowest. The tidal range is low, and such tides are called *neap tides*.

Tides That Are Different

Not all places on sea coasts have two high tides a day. Most places on the shores of the oceans do. But in some, the shape and depth of bays or seas prevents the second tide from rising very high, so that there appears to be only one high tide per day.

The tidal range in mid-ocean is not very large—about 3 feet (1 meter). But as high tide approaches the shore, the

If the moon stood still while the earth rotated, any given point on the earth would go from high water to low to high to low and back to high water in a 24-hour period.

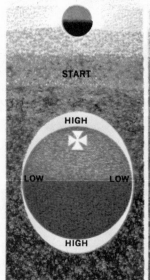
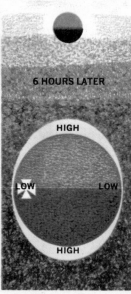
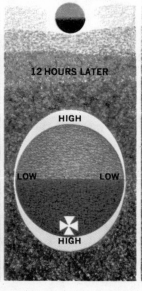
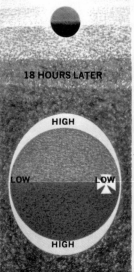
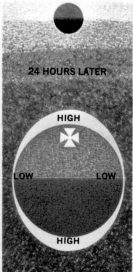

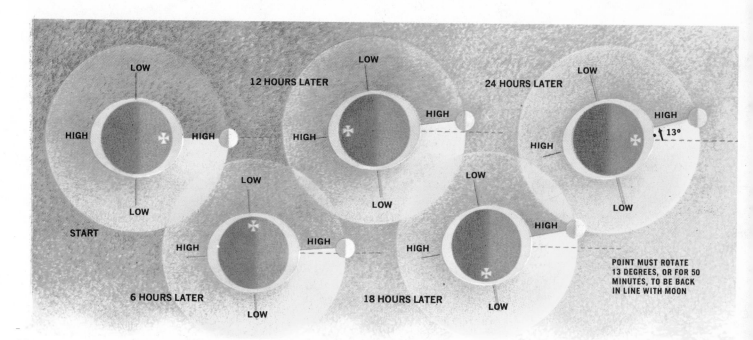

Because the moon does revolve round the earth (above), any given point goes from high water (directly opposite the moon) back to the same high-water position in 24 hours and 50 minutes. When the sun's gravitational pull is added to that of the moon (below), high tides are at their highest and low tides at their lowest. These are called spring tides. When the sun opposes the moon—at the moon's first and last quarters—the lowest high tides and the highest low tides occur. These are called neap tides.

SPRING TIDES

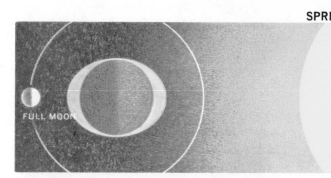
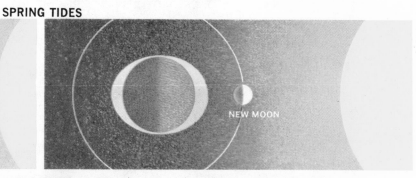

NEAP TIDES

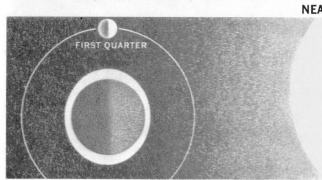

extra water tends to pile up. The tidal range increases to about 10 feet (3 meters) at the coast. In many places, the shape of the coastline funnels the water into a narrow bay and raises it even more. The greatest tides occur in the Bay of Fundy, in Canada, where the tide may rise and fall more than 50 feet (15 meters).

Tidal Bores

Where a large tidal range occurs, strong coastal currents may be set up as the tide rises and falls. In a few cases, the high tide is forced into the mouth of a river. At certain times, this causes a huge wall of water to move swiftly up the river. This moving wall is called a bore. Well-known bores occur on the River Severn in England, the Amazon in South America, and the Petitcodiac, which empties into the Bay of Fundy.

OCEAN CURRENTS

The oceans are also in constant movement because of the currents running through them. This movement of water around the globe helps us greatly. Because of the currents, warm water reaches cold regions, and cold water flows to warm regions. This helps to distribute the sun's heat all over the world. The currents also stir up the vast food stores in the ocean, carrying sea life to regions that would otherwise be lifeless.

The currents at the surface of the sea are blown by the winds, so the patterns of currents in the oceans follow the patterns of winds above them. The currents mainly flow northwards or southwards from the Equator, but the spinning of the earth throws them to the right in the Northern Hemisphere and to the left in the Southern Hemisphere. As a result, a few great circles of currents occupy the world's oceans. They swirl clockwise to the north of the Equator, and anti-clockwise to the south of the Equator.

At the Equator, there is a current that flows in the opposite direction to the circles, flowing east. It starts where some of the water from the great circular currents meets a coastline and turns back on itself. A great current, made up of the southern parts of the circles in the Southern Hemisphere, flows eastwards round the continent of Antarctica. It is called the West Wind Drift, because it is blown by winds called the westerlies, and it moves more water than any other current.

A tidal bore, a moving wall of water, sweeps along the Petitcodiac River.

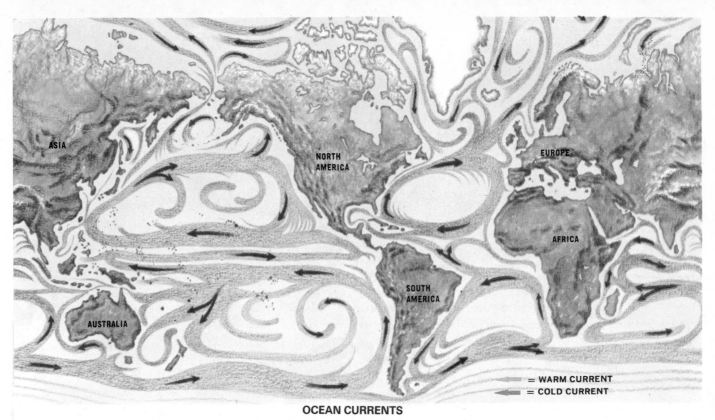

OCEAN CURRENTS

Warm and cold currents flow like great rivers within the oceans, so that the water in the sea is never still. Currents are usually started by wind blowing over the water.

The Gulf Stream

One of the world's best-known currents is the Gulf Stream. It starts in the Gulf of Mexico and flows northwards up the east coast of North America. Its warm blue waters are so different from the cold, grey-green waters to the north that the edges of the current can easily be seen. The effect of the earth's spinning sends the Gulf Stream out into the Atlantic and away from the North American coast. There it becomes the North Atlantic Drift. Its warm waters eventually reach the shores of Europe. They give the countries of western Europe a mild climate. But parts of North America at the same latitude (distance from the Equator) have very cold winters because the waters that wash their shores come from the Arctic Ocean and not from the tropics.

The great circular movement of the North Atlantic, of which the Gulf Stream and North Atlantic Drift form a major part, encloses an area of still water at its center. There huge quantities of sargassum, a kind of seaweed, drift in the still water and give the region its name, the Sargasso Sea.

Cold Currents From the Poles

Beneath the world's major surface currents, deeper currents of cold water flow from the polar regions. This polar water has a lot more living things in it than the warm tropical water, and in some places the cold water comes up to the surface. Where this occurs, the ocean is full of fish and other animals feeding in the rich cold water. The Humboldt Current, or Peru Current, is a cold current that starts in Antarctica and flows northwards along the western coast of South America. A vast number of fish live in the current, especially anchovies. As a result, fish and fish products are Peru's greatest export.

63

Climates of the World

When we talk about 'weather', we mean the amount of sunshine, wind, cloud, rain and warmth that an area experiences from day to day—or from hour to hour. Weather can change. One day it may be warm and sunny, the next it may be cold and rainy. 'Climate' means something rather different. It is the wide range of weather that an area experiences over a period of many years.

Whether we wear a raincoat and carry an umbrella on one day, or wear a light jacket and sunglasses the next, depends on the weather. But far more important things depend on climate. Different kinds of plants need different amounts of sun,

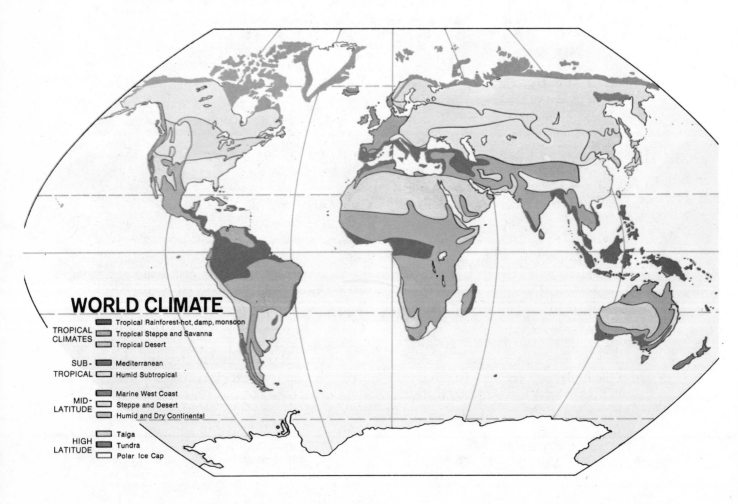

WORLD CLIMATE

TROPICAL CLIMATES
- Tropical Rainforest-hot, damp, monsoon
- Tropical Steppe and Savanna
- Tropical Desert

SUB-TROPICAL
- Mediterranean
- Humid Subtropical

MID-LATITUDE
- Marine West Coast
- Steppe and Desert
- Humid and Dry Continental

HIGH LATITUDE
- Taiga
- Tundra
- Polar Ice Cap

rain and warmth. So certain plants only grow in certain climates. Open and airy houses, with plenty of windows and perhaps a balcony or veranda, are best for warm climates. But for cold climates, homes must be snug and cosy. A people's traditional dress—even their way of life —depends on the climate of their country.

ELEMENTS AND CLIMATE

The various conditions that go to make one sort of climate (or weather) different from another are called elements. The two most important elements are temperature and *precipitation*. (Precipitation is the general name for all the forms— rain, snow, hail or sleet—in which water falls to the earth.) Other elements are humidity (moisture in the air), cloud, fog, sunshine, wind, storms and air pressure.

An area of land that shares the same elements and climate is called a climatic region. There are many ways in which we can tell them apart. The sun's heat is an important element of climate. So we generally describe an area's climate according to how far that area is from the Equator—the hottest part of the earth.

The parts of the earth above and below the Equator are known as the Northern and Southern Hemispheres. They are each divided into four main areas. The area around the Equator is called the tropics and has a tropical climate. Next come the cooler subtropical climates. After a narrow band of temperate climate come the cold climates and the polar climates.

THE TROPICS

Tropical climates are found in regions between latitudes 35° north and 35° south of the Equator: that is, in central Africa, Brazil and the islands to the north of Australia. In these areas, the temperature rarely falls below about 27 °C (80 °F). The weather is more or less the same all the year round. Winter is much like summer, autumn like spring. The tropics all have a great deal of sunlight and share similar temperatures. But there are differences from area to area.

These differences are due to differing amounts of rainfall and humidity. Some parts—such as the Amazon basin, in Brazil, and the Congo basin, in Africa— get a lot of rain all through the year. Warm rainstorms, with thunder and lightning, are common. This type of climate is called *tropical humid*. Because it is hot and wet all through the year, plants of all sorts grow quickly and cover the land with dense vegetation. The most common type of vegetation are the tropical rain forests, which cover huge areas on or near the Equator.

It is hottest near the Equator because there the heat from the sun's rays is spread over a small area.

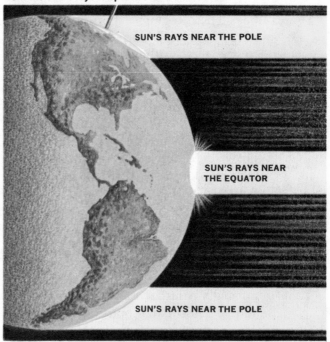

SUN'S RAYS NEAR THE POLE

SUN'S RAYS NEAR THE EQUATOR

SUN'S RAYS NEAR THE POLE

The Amazon basin has a tropical climate known as tropical humid. Heavy rainfalls throughout the year produce fast-growing, lush vegetation.

Lands a bit further away from the Equator (including parts of India and northern Australia) have a slightly different climate. This is called *tropical wet-and-dry*. It is still very hot, but each year brings a dry season as well as a rainy one. These regions experience a greater range in temperature from one season to the next, although it is never cold enough for frost to form at night. The forests are usually less dense than in tropical humid areas, and the trees often lose their leaves in the dry season. Parts of the tropics are drier still. Fewer trees grow in the tropical savannas. In the tropical deserts of Africa, America and Australia nothing grows at all.

HOT AND COLD

Next to the tropics (although normally separated from them by dry regions) lie the *sub-tropical* lands. They normally stretch between latitudes 30° and 40°, north and south of the Equator. The seasons in tropical climates differ (if they differ at all) only in the amount of rainfall. Sub-tropical areas, on the other hand, have definite seasons—hot summers and cool, even frosty, winters. Like the various tropical climates, sub-tropical climates can be dry or wet.

The dry sub-tropical climate is called the *Mediterranean* climate. Only one-fiftieth of the earth has this type of climate—perhaps the most pleasant of all. Apart from the Mediterranean region, it is to be found along the western coasts of sub-tropical land masses. These areas include the coast of California, central Chile, the tip of South Africa and parts of southern Australia.

The Mediterranean climate brings hot dry summers and mild, fairly rainy winters. Plants grow in abundance—especially fruits such as oranges, lemons and grapes. Most of the world's vineyards are in Mediterranean climates.

Sub-tropical humid climates are to be found on the eastern coasts of the continents. They bring a lot of rain—

especially in the hot summers—and some snow in winter. There is enough rainfall throughout the year for thick forests to grow. Cotton grows well and there are grasslands where cattle graze. Some sub-tropical humid regions are the eastern and southern coasts of the United States, Argentina, China and eastern Australia.

THE TEMPERATE ZONES

To the north and south of the sub-tropical climates, stretching between latitudes 40° to 55°, lie the cooler *temperate* zones. The climates in these areas are of two very different types: temperate oceanic and temperate continental.

A *temperate oceanic* climate is mild all the year round and brings moderate rainfall. It is found along the coasts of the continents—the Pacific coasts of North America and southern Chile, on the Atlantic coasts of northern Europe, and in New Zealand. Westerly winds blow for most of the year bringing the same amount of moisture during all the seasons. These winds also help to warm the lands in the winter, and cool them in the summer. The moist climate encourages plant growth. Temperate oceanic regions were once covered in thick forests. Most of these forests have now been replaced with grasslands, which support sheep and cattle.

Temperate continental climates occur at the same latitudes as temperate oceanic but usually at the center of continents, far from the oceans. They are to be found in central and eastern North America,

Spain and other countries bordering on the Mediterranean Sea have a dry sub-tropical climate.

Many of the world's largest cities are found in temperate oceanic climates, which are mild all the year round and have a moderate rainfall.

central and eastern Europe, and in parts of Asia. Oceanic winds do not travel this far. So summers are usually hot and winters freezing cold. A great deal of rain falls, however, and there is snow in winter. Grasslands once covered the land, but wheat and other crops are now grown. The great wheat-growing prairies of North America lie in temperate continental climates.

FROST AND ICE

In the freezing lands of Alaska, Siberia, parts of Canada and Scandinavia, grow vast coniferous forests. The climate there is cold. The winters are long, and temperatures in summer are barely above freezing. What little rain there is falls mainly in the summer. These regions, which stretch as far as the forests, have a *boreal*, or *subarctic*, climate.

Nearer to the poles, it is so cold that no trees can survive. These regions are called the tundra. The only form of life that can live in the tundra are grasses, mosses and lichens. Greenland, the Arctic and Antarctic have even colder climates. These are the lands of permanent ice and polar climates.

OTHER CLIMATES

The climate of any region depends on how much rain falls there. There are no set patterns of rainfall throughout the world, as there are of the strength of the sun's rays. As much—or as little—rain may fall in temperate and sub-tropical areas as in tropical wet-and-dry areas.

Deserts are to be found in all the climatic regions of the earth, especially in the middle of continents or behind mountain barriers. The deserts of Africa and Asia are dry because they are never reached by the rain-carrying winds that blow inland from the oceans. The deserts of North America are near to the Pacific ocean, but lie behind mountains too high for the rain-bearing winds of the Pacific to cross.

Altitude—that is, the height of the

Polar climates (above) are found in the Arctic, Antarctic and Greenland. Man-made canals (below) water the fields at Giza in Egypt; deserts have a very low rainfall and under natural conditions they have almost no vegetation.

The height of a mountain can influence the climate of an area. The mountains may have a permanent snow cap but the lower regions around it will be warm.

land—can have a great effect on an area's climate. The higher the area is above sea level, the lower its temperature will usually be. Thus Mount Fuji in Japan and Africa's Mount Kilimanjaro have permanent snow caps, while the lower areas surrounding them are warm.

Land and Water

Climates are also affected a great deal by seas and waters nearby. Water warms up—and cools down—much slower than land. Oceans are usually warmer in winter, and cooler in summer, than the land nearby. This makes the climate of the land moderate all the year round—cool in summer and mild in winter.

In many parts of the world, climate is affected by ocean currents that bring warm water to cool regions or cool water to hot areas. The Gulf Stream flows from the tropical Atlantic to the shores of north-west Europe, bringing with it warm waters and mild winter weather.

Winds and Mountains

Winds carry heat and moisture, and therefore affect climate. Winds that blow from lands in high latitudes (near the poles) are cold and dry. Winds from the sea are usually mild and wet. Some winds change direction with the seasons. In Asia, winds are dry and cool in the winter, when they blow from the land in the north. In the summer they blow from the seas of the south, bringing heavy rainfall and floods.

The direction of the winds is affected by mountain barriers. Air cools as it rises up the windward slopes of mountains (the side towards which the wind blows). As it does so, it gives up much of its moisture in the form of rain or snow. By the time the winds have crossed the mountains, they are dry. Areas on different sides of the mountains will thus have different climates. On one side they will be damp and rainy, and on the other side they will be dry.

Weather and Its Elements

The weather is a mixture of many different elements. Sunshine, rain, snow, fog and clouds are elements you can see. Temperature, wind and humidity (the moisture in the air) are elements you can feel. One element—air pressure—cannot be seen or felt. To test air pressure we need special measuring instruments.

These different elements are always at work. They bring days that are hot or cold, dry or wet, windy or calm. The moving air picks up moisture and heat as it sweeps over the earth's surface. The heat makes the air rise, and the moisture forms clouds, which the winds carry this way and that. The weather is a complicated mixture of many things. Some of these scientists understand, but others are still a mystery.

EARTH'S BLANKET OF AIR

The whole surface of the earth is surrounded by a blanket of air which we call the *atmosphere*. It is made up of several different gases and can hold various amounts of water vapor (water in gas form). At sea level the atmosphere normally presses down on the earth's surface with a pressure of about 14.7 pounds per square inch (1,033.5 grammes per square centimeter).

The atmosphere has four main layers. The highest is the *exosphere*, which starts at a height of about 650 miles (1,046 kilometers) and stretches farther out into space. Very little is known about the exosphere. Beneath it and stretching from 50 to 650 miles (80 to 1,046 kilometers) above the earth, is the *ionosphere*. This layer of the atmosphere acts as an electrical mirror. It bounces radio waves from one part of the earth to another.

The bottom two layers are the *stratosphere* and, beneath it, the *troposphere*. These are the two layers that affect our weather most. The stratosphere starts at heights of between 6 and 12 miles (10 and 20 kilometers) above the earth. Tempera-

---

WEATHER ELEMENTS

WEATHER ELEMENTS YOU CAN SEE:

- Rain
- Drizzle
- Hail
- Ice pellets

} Precipitation

- Clouds

- Fog
- Haze
- Smoke
- Dust
- Blowing dust, sand, or snow

} Restrictions to visibility (things that cut down your ability to see things at a distance)

- Water waves
- Rustling leaves
- Blowing dust, sand, or snow

} Effects of wind

WEATHER ELEMENTS YOU CAN FEEL:

- Temperature
- Dryness or dampness (humidity)
- Wind

WEATHER ELEMENTS YOU CAN MEASURE:

- Air pressure
- All the elements you can see or feel

What kind of clothing should you wear today? Perhaps this proposed method of weather forecasting would help you decide. If you saw the forecast at left on television, it would tell you the following: at 9 a.m. it will be overcast; the temperature will be −1°C; the winds will blow from the west at 15 kilometres per hour; there might be light snow or periods of rain. The number on the man's belt (2.4) tells you how warmly you should dress; a number 1 would indicate that you should wear a regular suit with the usual undergarments. Can you work out the forecasts for 12 noon, 3 p.m. and 6 p.m.?

tures there are always very low, and there is some wind and cloud.

The troposphere is where most of the world's active weather occurs. Most of the clouds, winds and storms are found in this layer. Rain and snow usually start there. The troposphere is about 4 or 5 miles (6 or 8 kilometers) thick over the cold lands of the poles. Over warmer areas, it stretches up to 11 or 12 miles (17 or 19 kilometers) above the surface of the earth. Temperatures at the bottom of the troposphere range from about 60° C (140° F) in desert regions to about −68° C (−90° F) at the poles.

Winds in the troposphere blow in all directions. There are currents of air that blow straight up and down. It is these vertical currents that lift moist air into higher regions where clouds form.

CLOUDY SKIES

Warm air can hold more water vapor than cold air. When air cools, the water in it condenses. In other words, it turns from a gas, or vapor, into a liquid. Clouds form when warm air rises from the earth's surface and becomes cool as it enters the colder regions above. As it cools, it sheds its moisture in the form of millions of tiny water droplets. These droplets are what clouds are made of. Scientists have worked out that about 100,000,000 of these droplets are needed to form a single large raindrop.

The coldest winter days occur when there are no clouds in the sky. This is because—strange though it may seem—clouds act as a blanket to keep the earth warm. They do this by letting the sun's rays pass through to warm the earth, while at the same time keeping in the heat that the earth normally reflects back into space. Clouds thus affect weather in more ways than simply as stores of rain or snow.

Supercooled Water and Ice

Some of the clouds we see on a cold winter day are made up of droplets of supercooled water. This is the name we give to water that does not turn to ice

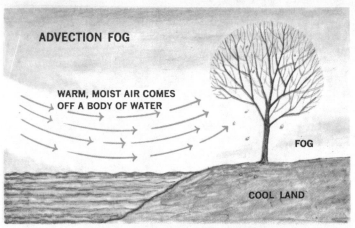

ADVECTION FOG

WARM, MOIST AIR COMES OFF A BODY OF WATER

FOG

COOL LAND

Fog is a cloud formation that stays close to the ground. The two main types of fog are advection fog (above) and radiation fog (below).

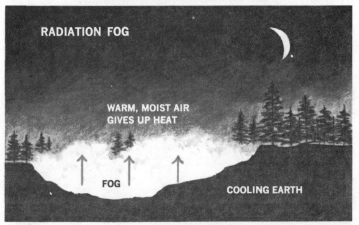

RADIATION FOG

WARM, MOIST AIR GIVES UP HEAT

FOG

COOLING EARTH

Static electricity builds up inside thunder clouds. When this happens, a giant spark—a lightning flash —jumps to another cloud or to the ground.

even though the temperature may be below freezing. Exactly why these water droplets stay in liquid form is still a mystery.

The thin, feathery clouds that can sometimes be seen floating high up in the atmosphere are of a different type. These are made up of ice crystals, instead of water droplets. The crystals are formed from supercooled droplets or straight from water vapor.

Types of Clouds

Cloud usually forms at heights of ½ to 7 miles (0.8 to 11 kilometers) above sea level. Cloud that is lower than this is usually called fog. Clouds come in many shapes and forms. They give the weatherman a good idea of the weather that lies ahead. There are three main groups of clouds—cumulus, stratus and cirrus.

Cumulus clouds are fluffy and cauliflower shaped, with broad, flat bases. They usually form over rapidly rising currents of warm air. They travel about 1 mile (1.6 kilometers) above the ground, often in groups of four or five. A great number of them together usually means rain.

Stratus clouds are thin, shapeless, foggy clouds. They can often be seen in early morning or late evening floating above columns of still, or slowly rising air. They usually occur only a few thousand feet up.

Cirrus are among the highest clouds of all. They are white and wispy and sometimes called 'mares' tails'. These usually drift along at heights of about 10 miles (16 kilometers), often in delicate patterns.

RAIN, SNOW, SLEET AND HAIL

Rain, snow, sleet and hail form from moisture in the air. The air picks up this

Fair-weather cumulus clouds.

Cirro-cumulus clouds make a 'mackerel sky'.

Stratus clouds stretch across the sky in grey layers.

Grey or bluish sheets of alto-stratus clouds.

Thin, lacy cirrus clouds are made of ice crystals.

Cirro-stratus clouds cause a halo round the moon.

**Above: Strato-cumulus clouds loosely packed.
Below: Alto-cumulus clouds with thin edges of layers.**

Above: Nimbo-stratus clouds are low, thick rain clouds. Below: Cumulo-numbus are storm clouds.

moisture as it sweeps over oceans, rivers and lakes. The warmer the air is, the more moisture it can carry. Sooner or later the warm, moist air rises. As it rises, it cools. And as it cools, it gives up its moisture. Then tiny water droplets—or ice crystals —form.

These particles of water or ice are at first so tiny and light that they are carried this way and that by the winds. Countless millions of these particles gathered together form clouds. Then, if conditions are right, these droplets or ice particles start to stick together. This process goes on until many millions of the droplets have come together to form what we know as a raindrop or hail stone. These particles are heavy—too heavy to be carried along by the winds—so they fall out of the clouds and drop down to the earth.

Many millions of water droplets gathered together fall as raindrops. Ice crystals fall as snow. Sometimes the water freezes or the ice melts on its way down. This happens if the particle has to pass through cooler or warmer layers of air on its journey to the ground. Frozen rain is called hail. Hail sometimes falls even on a warm summer's day; this shows that it is freezing cold high up in the sky. Melted snow—or snow that has only partly melted—reaches the ground in a form known as sleet.

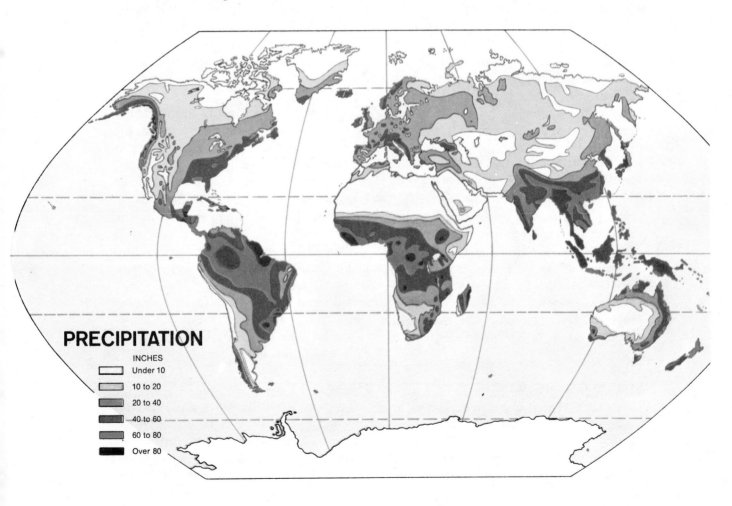

PRECIPITATION

INCHES
Under 10
10 to 20
20 to 40
40 to 60
60 to 80
Over 80

Snowflakes magnified many times. Each snowflake is made up of a number of ice crystals, and no two snowflakes have exactly the same shape.

Rain Round the World

The wettest areas of the earth are on or near the Equator. Round the Equator there is a band of warm, moist air that is always rising. As it rises, it sheds its water and rain falls. Other parts of the world, such as the deserts of Asia, Africa and America, get very little rain. The wettest place in the world is Mt. Waialeale, in Hawaii. The average yearly rainfall there is 460 inches (11,684 millimeters). The driest place is the Atacama Desert in Chile. In one part of this desert, no rain has fallen for hundreds of years.

Many things determine how much rain or snow an area receives. Mountain barriers can attract rain or keep it off. An area's temperature or altitude (height above sea level) can also affect rainfall. But perhaps the most important single factor is wind.

THE BLOWING WINDS

The air is always in motion. The main reason for this is heat. It is due to heat, or the lack of it, that some air is light and rises, while other air is heavy and sinks.

The hottest part of the earth is the Equator. The air there is always being warmed, and is always rising. At the frosty North and South poles, air is cooled down and sinks. These two processes—thousands of miles apart as they may be—are closely linked. For the warm air rising at the Equator begins to travel high in the atmosphere to the poles in the north and south. The cool air that sinks at the poles gradually makes its way, travelling low over the ground, to the Equator. A moving circle of air is set up, travelling over the whole face of the earth.

This north–south passage of air is broken up into a number of smaller patterns, or cells, of moving air. Most of the world's winds blow from east or west because the general movement of air between Equator and poles is affected by the earth's spinning movement.

Highs and Lows

The weight of the air usually measures almost 15 pounds per square inch at the bottom of the atmosphere. But at the Equator, air is rising—and weighs less. Meteorologists express this by saying that

In a high-pressure area the strongest winds (shown by the heaviest arrows) blow round the edges. In a low-pressure area, the strongest winds are near the center.

there is a belt of low pressure at the Equator. At the poles, where air is falling, air weighs more. The poles are therefore areas of high pressure.

Areas of high and low pressure, usually many hundreds of miles in diameter, are to be found scattered over much of the earth's surface. The other elements are always at work, producing new ones. They may travel many thousands of miles before gradually disappearing. Areas of low pressure are generally called *cyclones*. High pressure areas are called *anticyclones*.

Cyclones bring very windy, stormy weather. In the temperate zones—in western Europe, for example—large cyclonic storms bring a day or two of rain or snow until the cyclone passes on.

Other parts of the world, such as the warm parts of America and Asia, have a different type of cyclonic storm—the *tornado*. Tornadoes may last only a few minutes. But the winds are so strong that they can blow a railway train off its tracks or tear the roof off a house.

Over tropical oceans, lows can grow to 300 or 400 miles (483 to 644 kilometers) in diameter, with winds of up to 200 miles (322 kilometers) an hour. Such a storm is called a *hurricane* in the Atlantic. The Asian name for it is a *typhoon*.

Highs, or anticyclones, usually bring light winds and fair weather. But in some parts of the world, they may be very unpleasant. In dry areas, long-lasting highs can cause droughts. In warm coastal regions, highs may bring warm, moist air that can be very unpleasant. Highs, like lows, normally move in a west-to-east direction.

HOW THE WEATHER WORKS

Winds always blow from areas of high pressure to areas of low pressure. They bring with them masses of air, which may be warm or cold, wet or dry. Winds do not blow into areas of high pressure, and so these areas have steady and unchanging weather.

When two air masses containing different kinds of air meet, a *front* forms between them. If the cold air is moving faster than the warm air, a cold front forms. If the warm air is moving faster, we have a warm front. But in both cases the warm air rises and the two air masses pass one on top of the other. The warm air that rises becomes cooler. As it sheds its moisture clouds form. This causes

rain to fall and there may even be thunderstorms.

The boundary between the two air masses is always sloped. But a cold front has a steeper slope than a warm front. As a result, the weather from a cold front may be very stormy, but it never lasts more than a day or so. When the front has passed, the rain stops and the clouds disappear. The winds die down and the temperature drops. A warm front may bring rain for several days.

STUDYING THE WEATHER

Meteorologists must study the weather carefully and make certain measurements before they can foretell the weather to come. Meteorological stations containing measuring instruments are now operating all over the world. Their observations are recorded daily.

The instruments that are used to mea-

Above: In a cold front, the cold air mass pushes under a warm air mass. Below: A warm front is broader than a cold front. It forms when a warm air mass slides over a cold air mass.

RELATIVE HUMIDITY TABLE

DRY-BULB MINUS WET-BULB TEMPERATURE	DRY-BULB TEMPERATURE								RELATIVE HUMIDITY IN PERCENT
	30	40	50	60	70	80	90	100	
0	•	•	•	•	•	•	•	•	100
1									
2	•	•	•	•	•	•	•	•	90
3									
4	•	•	•	•	•	•	•	•	80
5									
6									
7									
8	•	•	•	•	•	•	•	•	70
9									
10	•	•	•	•	•	•	•	•	60
12									
14	•	•	•	•	•	•	•	•	50
16									
18									
20	•	•	•	•	•	•	•	•	40
25	•	•	•	•	•	•	•	•	30
30									20
35	•	•	•	•	•	•	•	•	10
40	•	•	•	•	•	•	•	•	5
45	•	•	•	•	•	•	•	•	0

Above: In the relative humidity table, the column at the left represents the difference between a wet- and dry-bulb reading. The figures at the top represent dry-bulb readings. Find the figures closest to yours and read down from the dry-bulb figure and across from the difference between the wet- and dry-bulb figures. Find the dot that is in line with both. Then follow the coloured band to the right to find the relative humidity. Below: A psychrometer is an instrument that measures humidity.

sure the weather are quite simple. Sunshine recorders measure sunshine by focusing the sun's rays on a card. As the sun moves through the sky, its path is recorded in burn-marks on the card. An area's rainfall is measured by putting out a bottle, fitted with a funnel to collect rain. The rainfall—the depth of water produced by the rain—is measured in inches or millimeters. Humidity—the proportion of water vapor in the air—is another important factor to be recorded. This is measured by first taking the temperature of the air with a thermometer. Then another reading is made with the thermometer wrapped in a wet cloth. The *wet-bulb thermometer* will give a lower temperature, due to the coolness of the evaporating moisture. Humidity can be worked out from the two temperature readings.

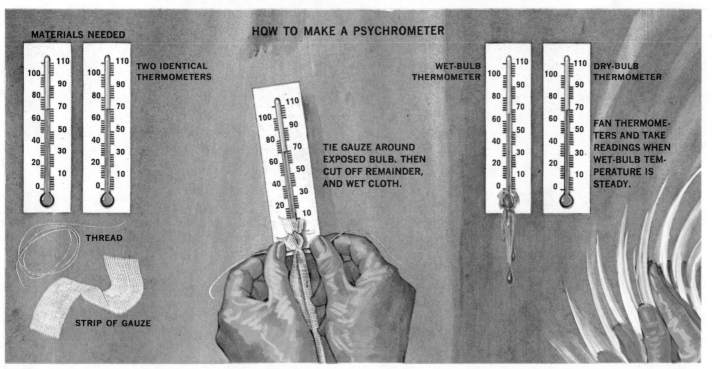

HOW TO MAKE A PSYCHROMETER

MATERIALS NEEDED

TWO IDENTICAL THERMOMETERS

THREAD

STRIP OF GAUZE

TIE GAUZE AROUND EXPOSED BULB. THEN CUT OFF REMAINDER, AND WET CLOTH.

WET-BULB THERMOMETER

DRY-BULB THERMOMETER

FAN THERMOMETERS AND TAKE READINGS WHEN WET-BULB TEMPERATURE IS STEADY.

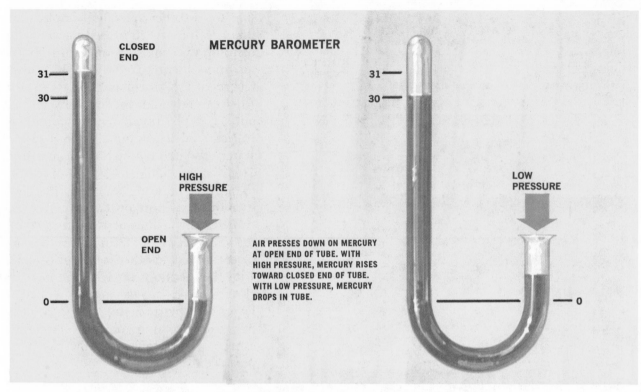

A mercury barometer is often used by meteorologists to measure atmospheric pressure.

Ordinary air temperature must be measured regularly—and so must the weight, or pressure, of the air. Air pressure is measured by an instrument called a *barometer*. This works by balancing the weight of the air against the weight of a column of mercury in a tube. Wind speed and direction is measured with an instrument called an *anemometer*. This is also used to measure the amount and kind of cloud to be seen.

In recent years, meterologists have been helped by unmanned, high-flying balloons, and weather satellites orbiting the earth. Balloons and satellites carry cameras to photograph the cloud below. They also have instruments to measure temperatures on the earth's surface. Radar is widely used in weather forecasting to detect distant rain showers and storms.

These modern aids enable the meteorologist to look at the world's weather at a glance and see how weather systems are developing.

Weather Maps

When the weatherman has collected all these bits of information, he draws a map of the area he is studying and writes in all the information he has gathered. There are many different types of weather maps, but the most common is the synoptic map. This gives a general picture of the sort of weather an area can expect to get in one or two days' time.

First, the meteorologist draws in lines called *isobars*, which connect all the points where air pressure is the same. When he has drawn several of these lines, a rough circle begins to appear round the centers

BEAUFORT SCALE OF WIND VELOCITIES			
BEAUFORT NUMBER	WIND DESCRIPTION	VELOCITY (IN MILES PER HOUR)	EFFECT OF WIND
0	CALM	BELOW 1	NO PERCEPTIBLE MOVEMENT; SMOKES RISES VERTICALLY
1	LIGHT AIR	1 TO 3	LEAVES MOVE SLIGHTLY; WIND DIRECTION SHOWN BY DRIFT OF SMOKE
2	LIGHT BREEZE	4 TO 7	LEAVES RUSTLE; WIND FELT ON FACE
3	GENTLE BREEZE	8 TO 12	LEAVES AND TWIGS IN CONSTANT MOTION; WIND EXTENDS LIGHTWEIGHT FLAG
4	MODERATE BREEZE	13 TO 18	SMALL BRANCHES MOVE; DUST AND LOOSE PAPER ARE DRIVEN ALONG GROUND
5	FRESH BREEZE	19 TO 24	SMALL LEAFY TREES BEGIN TO SWAY
6	STRONG BREEZE	25 TO 31	LARGE TREE BRANCHES IN CONSTANT MOTION; WHISTLING HEARD IN TELEGRAPH WIRES
7	MODERATE GALE	32 TO 38	WHOLE TREES IN MOTION; INCONVENIENCE IN WALKING
8	FRESH GALE	39 TO 46	TWIGS AND SMALL BRANCHES BREAK; DIFFICULT TO WALK
9	STRONG GALE	47 TO 54	MAN-MADE STRUCTURES SLIGHTLY DAMAGED
10	WHOLE GALE	55 TO 63	TREES UPROOTED; CONSIDERABLE STRUCTURAL DAMAGE OCCURS
11	STORM	64 TO 75	WIDESPREAD DAMAGE
12	HURRICANE	OVER 75	SEVERE AND EXTENSIVE DAMAGE

Above: The Beaufort wind scale, which can be used in keeping records of wind speeds. Below: Weather stations use an instrument called an anemometer to measure wind speed.

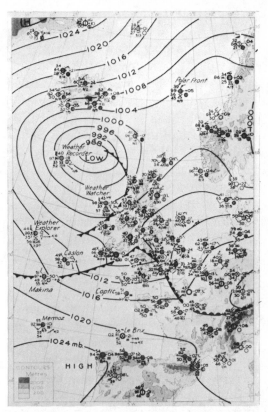

A weather map generally shows high and low pressure areas and any warm or cold fronts that may be moving over the region. It also shows whether rain, snow or fog can be expected, the humidity, temperature and wind speed.

of high and low pressure areas. Then he marks in the warm or cold fronts that may be moving over the area. He will already know about the fronts from earlier observations, since they generally move slowly.

When he has finished with patterns of air pressure and fronts, the meteorologist shades in areas of rain, snow and fog. He then adds figures to mark such things as humidity, temperature and wind speed. The map is now complete. By comparing it with maps produced from earlier observations, the meteorologist can make a good guess about the weather that is to come.

WEATHER CONTROL

Knowing what the weather will be like can help farmers tend their crops, airplane pilots to avoid storms, and ships at sea to travel in greater safety. But it cannot stop disasters such as droughts or floods; nor can it lessen the damage caused by hailstorms, hurricanes or tornadoes. To do this, the weather itself must be changed.

The scientists of many countries have tried—with some success—to take rain or snow out of clouds by a method known as 'seeding'. Scientists are still not sure exactly how raindrops and snowflakes form. But it seems likely that they form when millions of tiny water droplets or ice crystals gather round particles of dust, salt, smoke or some other floating particle. When a certain number of these droplets or ice crystals have come together, they fall to earth as raindrops or snowflakes. If the air in the cloud is completely free of dust particles, no rain or snow can fall.

Scientists have tried to find substances to take the place of dust particles. They have found that ice crystals can be made to gather round silver iodide crystals or 'dry ice' (particles of carbon dioxide in solid form). Snow has fallen many times after clouds have been seeded in this way by planes carrying cargoes of dry ice and silver iodide.

Warm clouds—containing water droplets rather than ice crystals—have been seeded in similar ways. A cargo of 400 gallons (1,818 liters) of water, sprayed from a plane, has produced rain inside a cloud. No rain actually fell, but the water droplets within the cloud did gather together to produce rain.

It may be that, in a few years' time, scientists will be able to turn rainfall on and off like a tap, and tame the wildest storms by seeding. But much more has to be found out about the natural conditions that can help turn water droplets into raindrops, and allow them to fall to the earth below.

A cloud, after being seeded with dry ice. Seeding causes rain or snow to fall.

The Earth's Blanket of Air

Our planet is surrounded by a blanket of air that stretches from its surface into outer space for a distance of several hundred miles. This blanket of air is called the atmosphere. We depend on it for our existence. Among other things, it contains two gases—oxygen and carbon dioxide—that all living things must have. The atmosphere also helps protect the earth from ultra-violet radiation, cosmic rays and meteors.

The atmosphere is important in other ways, too. It keeps the earth warm as it circles in the biting cold of outer space. And it helps to spread heat from one part of the earth to another, so that the earth can support life over most of its surface. The atmosphere carries sound waves and allows various forms of radiation such as heat, light and radio waves to reach us. Without some of these, we would die.

Ancient thinkers knew how important air was. Some thought it was a living thing, regarding it as a spirit or a god. We know today that the earth's atmosphere is neither alive nor divine. But we can understand why people believed as they did.

WHAT IS THE ATMOSPHERE?

The atmosphere is made up of a number of different gases. Some are heavy, and cling close to the earth's surface; others are light and make up the highest part of the atmosphere, where it touches outer space. Some of these gases always exist in the same proportions. These are the permanent atmospheric gases. Others vary in quantity from place to place and from time to time. These are called variable gases.

There are 10 permanent atmospheric gases. Most of them exist in such small quantities that we can disregard them. The two most important are nitrogen and oxygen. Nitrogen makes up over three-quarters of the air we breathe. Oxygen accounts for a little more than one-fifth of the entire atmosphere.

Oxygen is one of the gases of the atmosphere that helps to make the earth a living planet. Our lungs take oxygen out of every breath of air we take. Our bodies use it to turn food into energy. Our need for nitrogen is less obvious, but indirectly this gas is just as precious as oxygen. Plants take nitrogen from the soil. And animals, including man, feed on the plants or on other animals that eat the plants.

Two other permanent gases—hydrogen and helium—are found in very small amounts in areas near the earth's surface, but make up much of the higher regions of the atmosphere.

Important variable gases of the atmosphere are carbon dioxide, water vapor and a special form of oxygen called ozone. Water vapor is water in the form of gas. It is found only in the lower part of the atmosphere and makes up about one-tenth of the atmosphere. As air sweeps

180 MI.

170 MI.

160 MI.

150 MI.

140 MI.

130 MI.

120 MI.

110 MI.

100 MI.

90 MI.

80 MI.

70 MI.

60 MI.

50 MI.

40 MI.

30 MI.

20 MI.

10 MILES

ULTRAVIOLET AND X RAYS

ASTRONAUT CAPSULE

AURORA BOREALIS

SHORT RADIO WAVES

METEOR TRAILS

MANNED ROCKET PLANE

OZONE LAYER

MANNED BALLOON

TROPOPAUSE

½ OF ATMOSPHERE BELOW THIS LINE

MT. EVEREST (5 MILES)

GREATEST OCEAN DEPTH (7 MILES)

+3000° F.

+1000° F.

+80° F.

−40° F.

+20° F.

−70° F.

+70° F.

IONOSPHERE

MESOSPHERE

STRATOSPHERE

TROPOSPHERE

over water surfaces—oceans, lakes and rivers—it takes in water vapor. When conditions are right the water falls to earth again in the form of rain.

Carbon dioxide occurs in tiny amounts, but it is as necessary as oxygen to life on earth. Green plants use it in a process called photosynthesis, by which they make their food and give off oxygen as a waste product.

Ozone exists in greater or lesser amounts over the whole surface of the globe, but is more common over green country and high ground. It soaks up much of the harmful ultra-violet radiation that bombards the earth from the sun.

In addition, the lower atmosphere is full of countless tiny particles of matter—soil, salt and specks of dust from burned materials and plants. Some of these particles can be seen floating in the air when light from a sunbeam falls on them. Water droplets gather round these particles to form clouds.

HOW AIR BEHAVES

Air is matter just as rocks are. Like all matter, it is pulled by the earth's gravity. This means that it has weight. Scientists say that, if all of the earth's atmosphere could be collected together and weighed, it would weigh about 5,700,000,000,000,000 tons.

We refer to the weight of the air when we talk about air pressure. We measure air pressure by measuring the force with which the air presses down on a square inch of the earth's surface. At sea level, where air pressure is greatest, it presses

The layers of the atmosphere absorb solar radiations in different ways. As a result, the temperatures of the layers are different. For example, the upper layer of the stratosphere, called the mesosphere, is very cold because its thin air does not absorb ultra-violet rays from the sun.

down with a force of 14·7 pounds per square inch. This can also be expressed as a force of about 1,033·5 grammes on each square centimeter.

The air presses down not only on the earth but also on water, plants, our bodies and everything else. And it does not only press down, although this is how we normally express it. It presses against all surfaces from below and from the sides as well as from above. It presses on every inch of skin of your body. The total weight of air pressure on your whole body is about one ton.

As we go higher, the air pressure becomes less. It is less on a mountain top than it is at sea level. And it is less in a high-flying aircraft than on a mountain top. That is why some aircraft are designed to maintain normal air pressure inside while flying at heights where the air pressure outside is very low.

LAYER UPON LAYER

Our atmosphere is made up of several layers, each one different from the others. The main layers are the troposphere, the stratosphere, the ionosphere and the exosphere.

The Troposphere in Which We Live

The bottom layer of the atmosphere is called the troposphere. This varies in thickness, depending on the temperature of the earth below. At the equator it is about 12 miles (19.3 kilometers) thick, but at the North and South Poles it is only 4 miles (6.4 kilometers) thick.

About half the earth's atmosphere is squeezed into the bottom 3.5 miles (5.6 kilometers) of the troposphere by the weight of the air above it. And this is about the limit that man can ascend without a pressure suit and an oxygen mask.

The troposphere is where most of the earth's surface weather is formed. The winds circulate there, picking up water vapor which forms clouds and falls back to earth as rain. Winds blow in every direction over the earth's surface, while currents of air rise and fall, creating areas of low and high pressure on the earth's surface.

Balloons that carry measuring equipment through the troposphere show that the temperature falls steadily between the bottom and top of the troposphere. For each 1,000 feet (305 meters) of height, the temperature falls about 1·9°C (3·5°F). At the top of the troposphere the temperature falls to about −55·5°C (−70°F). This is because the sun's rays, although they pass through the atmosphere, do not warm it directly. They warm the earth below, and the earth in turn warms the air. Thus the air that is nearest to the earth is always warmer than the air high above.

The area where the troposphere ends—the tropopause—is where winds blow strongest. Most of the fast-moving winds called jet streams are found there. They flow along regular paths at speeds of up to 300 miles (480 kilometers) per hour.

The Clear, Dry Stratosphere

Beyond the tropopause lies the earth's second atmospheric layer—the stratosphere. There the air is dry, clear and icy cold, with winds sweeping across the lower regions. The air is also thinner than the air in the troposphere below. To balloonists and pilots of high-flying aircraft, the sky seems black and the stars shine brightly 24 hours a day.

In the middle of the stratosphere, between 12 and 22 miles (19.3 and 35.4 kilometers) above the earth's surface, lies a still layer of ozone. This gas absorbs most of the ultra-violet rays of the sun. Above the ozone layer, the temperature suddenly falls and the air becomes much thinner. At about 30 miles (48 kilometers) above the earth's surface, the stratosphere starts to merge with the next layer—the ionosphere. This layer, where the two merge, is called the mesosphere; it is actually the upper part of the stratosphere.

The Electrically Charged Ionosphere

Now we come to a very different layer in the atmosphere. The atoms and molecules of gas in the thin air of the ionosphere are bombarded by radiations from the sun. They are broken into smaller, electrically charged particles. In scientific language, such particles are said to be excited or disturbed. What it means is that electric currents can flow easily through the ionosphere.

It also means that the ionosphere acts as a huge mirror that reflects or sends back radio waves. This makes it very valuable for short-wave radio communication between points that are far apart. Radio waves go out in a straight line and cannot be made to bend round the curve of the earth. So ordinarily, a message beamed from, say, Europe to North America, would travel straight on into space. But what actually happens is that it hits the ionosphere and bounces back at an angle to North America.

The ionosphere is very hot. At 150 miles (240 kilometers) above the earth, temperatures may reach about 1,650°C (3,000°F). At night these temperatures may drop to about 1,100°C (2,000°F).

Exosphere: On the Edge of Space

About 300 miles (480 kilometers) above the earth, the gases get so thin that there is hardly any air resistance to a moving body. There, individual molecules may escape from the earth's gravitational pull and collide with the molecules of gases that may occur in space between the planets. Traces of such gases have been found 5,000 miles (8,000 kilometers) out in space.

ATMOSPHERE BRINGS LIGHT

In addition to protecting us from radiation and keeping us warm, the earth's atmosphere is helpful in other ways as well. One of the important functions that we often take for granted is its ability to spread light to places that would otherwise be inky black. Blue skies and brilliant sunsets are both effects of the atmosphere.

White light contains all the colors of the rainbow. And as the white rays of the sun pass through the gases and dust of the atmosphere they are broken up and scattered into colors. Blues and violets are usually more scattered than the other colors, so, as a result, the sky looks blue.

The sun's light near the horizon passes through many tiny specks of dust in the atmosphere. These specks absorb or take in several colors. The colors that get through are the oranges and reds of sunset and sunrise. If there happens to be a lot of moisture in the atmosphere when the sun is shining brightly, the particles of moisture break up the sunlight into all its colors. The result is what we call a rainbow.

RIDDLES OF THE ATMOSPHERE

There is still much to learn about our atmosphere. How do jet streams work and how do they affect our climate and weather? How are gases exchanged between layers? These and other puzzles have yet to be solved. But today scientists, as never before, have the tools to explore the atmosphere and so reach a greater understanding of it.

The Pollution of Our Planet

The earth supports life because it has plentiful supplies of air and water, and because the temperature—over most of its surface—is just right for living things. These living things live in a very delicate balance of life and death. Fish, plants, animals and man himself can all live together only because each helps the others to exist. Animals, for example, need oxygen to survive. In each breath they take oxygen out of the air and add carbon dioxide, as a waste product, to it. But this same carbon dioxide is needed by the plants of the world. In a process called photosynthesis, they take carbon dioxide out of the air and replace it with oxygen.

This is how life on earth has developed.

All living things—plants and animals—help each other to live by exchanging materials: they live in natural balance. By polluting the environment, man has upset this balance.

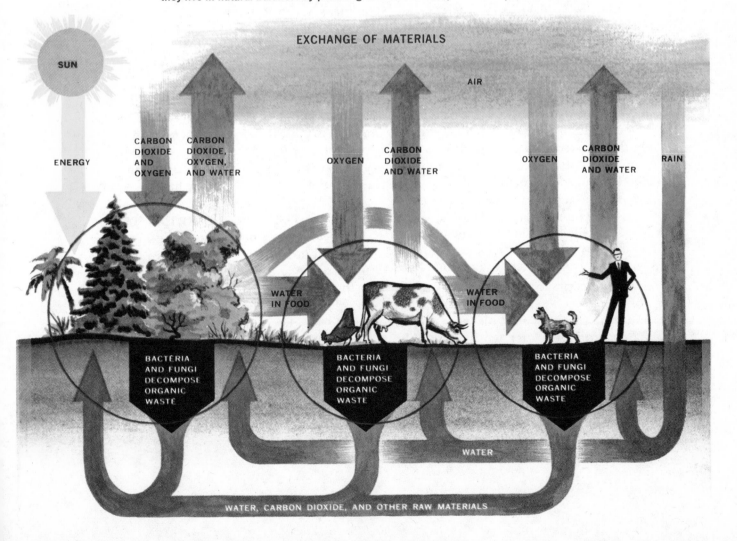

EXCHANGE OF MATERIALS

SUN

AIR

ENERGY

CARBON DIOXIDE AND OXYGEN

CARBON DIOXIDE, OXYGEN, AND WATER

OXYGEN

CARBON DIOXIDE AND WATER

OXYGEN

CARBON DIOXIDE AND WATER

RAIN

WATER IN FOOD

WATER IN FOOD

BACTERIA AND FUNGI DECOMPOSE ORGANIC WASTE

BACTERIA AND FUNGI DECOMPOSE ORGANIC WASTE

BACTERIA AND FUNGI DECOMPOSE ORGANIC WASTE

WATER

WATER, CARBON DIOXIDE, AND OTHER RAW MATERIALS

Man spreads thousands of tons of rubbish over the earth's surface every year.

And it has taken many millions of years. But in the last hundred years or so, man has begun to interfere with the earth's natural processes.

MAN THE POLLUTER

In 1800 the world's human population was about 1,000,000,000. It had taken about a million years to reach that figure. In those days man had little effect on the workings of the earth. But improved food supplies and man's ability to cure his illnesses and diseases have helped to increase the number of people in the world to over 4,000,000,000. In the next 30 years, this number will almost double. Man has also learned to use machines and build industries to make his life easier and more enjoyable. But his machines and industries all burn fuel and use oxygen. They produce wastes which cannot be used by the earth's animals and plants, but instead pile up all round us. Each of these man-made wastes is called a pollutant or, generally, pollution.

Man's activities are polluting the earth in many ways. Rubbish—used food cans, wrecked cars and other solid wastes— is one form of pollutant. Dirty water and air are another form. Man also produces more heat, noise and radiation than occur naturally: these are yet another form of pollutant. Pollution must be reduced if the earth is to survive. Otherwise the whole earth will change so greatly that, at some time in the future, it will not be able to support life.

DIRT IN THE AIR WE BREATHE

A person breathes about once every three seconds. About 30,000 times a day, air rushes in and out of our lungs. Some of the impurities that the air contains are absorbed by the body. Others are deposited on the walls of the lungs until, from their natural and healthy pink color, they become a dirty grey.

Winds and air currents usually help to spread the dirt over a large area, and rain and snow help to keep the air clean.

Air pollution in cities (left) is made worse by temperature inversion, when cool polluted air (above) is trapped under a layer of warm air.

But there are certain atmospheric conditions that can make the problem of pollution worse. One such condition is called a *temperature inversion*. In an inversion, cold and polluted air is trapped under a layer of warm air. The amount of pollution in the lower, colder air—which is the air that is breathed in—can build up to dangerous levels. Inversions most often occur over coastal cities, such as Los Angeles. There the pollution reaches such levels that people cannot see for more than a mile around them.

Man is the greatest cause of pollution. But some forms of air pollution can occur naturally. Each time a volcano erupts or a forest catches fire, clouds of dust and ash are spread for miles around.

The damage caused by air pollution is enormous. The smoke and gases produced by factories and automobiles kill plants, poison cattle, attack stonework and endanger health. The deadliest types of pollution cannot be seen at all. But even the smoke that rises from factory chimneys can become a killer. In London during the winter of 1952, smoke and fog joined to envelop the city for 4 days in a thick grey 'smog'. Within one month almost 4,000 people died of lung and heart failure. Parliament quickly passed a measure to cut down on smoke. Today London is smog-free.

Particles in the Air

Whenever two surfaces come together —such as a shoe on a pavement or car tires on a road surface—tiny particles of dust are thrown up into the air. Activities such as quarrying, drilling and paint-spraying send out more of these particles.

Fine particles of metal—zinc, cadmium, lead and others—pour out of factory chimneys. Each explosion of gasoline in a car engine produces particles of lead. Smoke itself—from burning oil, wood or coal—is made up of millions of particles. They stay floating in the air until rain or snow carries them down to the earth's surface.

All these impurities can be deadly—especially to people with weak lungs or hearts. But some of these poisons work in less obvious ways. Lead, for example, is a poison which can cause headaches, loss of appetite and severe tiredness. In greater quantities it can cause paralysis, bring on fits and destroy cells in the brain. Scientists have discovered that people who live near busy roads have more lead in their bodies than there should normally be. They have breathed in the lead in car exhaust. This lead has passed into the bloodstream and has started to collect in their bodies.

Gases in the Air

The most common gas pollutant is carbon monoxide—colorless and tasteless. It is produced whenever any fuel is burnt in a limited supply of air, such as petrol in a car engine. When breathed in, it reacts with the blood and stops it carrying oxygen round the body. An engine running in a garage will produce enough carbon monoxide in five minutes to kill a man. On busy city streets, enough may collect to cause tiredness and headaches—and perhaps interfere with a person's driving ability.

Another common—and dangerous—pollutant is sulphur dioxide. This is produced whenever sulphur is burnt, and sulphur forms a part of most fuels. Like carbon monoxide, it is colourless, but it has a distinctive smell—sweet and sharp. This is what you can smell when you strike a match, and it is the smell of a smoky town in winter.

Sulphur dioxide is harmful to many

Every time a jet takes off it sprays the air with polluting gases. The noise of jets can also damage buildings and cause us physical discomfort.

plants—including cotton, grapes and garden plants such as chrysanthemums and violets. It is also dangerous to people who breathe it, especially if they already suffer from lung diseases such as asthma or bronchitis. It was sulphur dioxide that killed the 4,000 victims of the London smog in 1952.

Sulphur dioxide is very dangerous because it mixes with oxygen to produce sulphur trioxide. This, in turn, combines with rainwater to form sulphuric acid. This acid attacks most of the materials we depend on. Metals, textiles and even stone are all destroyed by sulphuric acid. The stone of the Parthenon, Athens' ancient temple, has been damaged more in the last 50 years (by the sulphur dioxide produced by the factories and traffic of modern Athens)

than in its previous 2,500-year history.

Sulphur dioxide and carbon monoxide are just two of the most common pollutants. There are many others. Hydrogen sulphide—another gas that attacks metals—collects in large quantities round coal-gas factories. Car engines are responsible for a great deal of the pollution in our modern world. They produce various mixtures of nitrogen and oxygen, which in themselves cause lung diseases. In strong sunlight these oxides of nitrogen combine with other exhaust gases—the hydrocarbons left over from unburnt fuel—to produce what is called photochemical smog.

Fighting Air Pollution

Industrial countries throughout the world realize the importance of control-

Cars give off carbon monoxide, a dangerous gas, and are a major cause of air pollution.

Factories and plants have been serious sources of air pollution. Clouds of smoke and dust pour from two stacks of a steel plant (left). When special control devices are installed, industrial smoke is reduced or eliminated (right).

ling air pollution. Many of them now have some kind of control over the wastes that are pumped into their skies. But the factories and cars of the United States, for example, still produce one ton of pollution for every American citizen every year.

Pollution is most noticeable in cities and industrial areas. This is especially so if mountains or temperature inversions stop the dirty air from escaping. But the problem is also spreading to country areas. All the pollutants that enter the air must come down to earth sooner or later. High chimneys spread pollutants over a wide area, but can not make them disappear. Scientists in Sweden think that the increasing acidity of their rain is caused by the sulphur dioxide given off by factories in England—700 miles (1,126 kilometers) away.

The main causes of air pollution to-day are cars and other forms of transport, factories and power stations, and home heating systems. Clean Air Acts have been passed in England and in other countries. These and many international conferences have tried to get to grips with the problem of industrial air pollution. Britain's Act made householders and factories use smokeless fuel. By doing so, it gave many areas of the country the first clear skies they had seen for many years. Towns and cities are now cleaner places. But, as the Swedish scientists have found, the amount of sulphur dioxide has not fallen. The problem, as in many other areas of pollution control, is money. To get rid of air pollution completely would require costly new equipment as well as new methods of manufacturing all the products we use.

The United States, where cars are bigger and more numerous than anywhere else, is leading the fight against air pollution caused by automobiles. A law

Rubbish and other waste matter in many streams make it impossible for the water to support life.

passed in 1970 said that car manufacturers had to cut down by 90 per cent the hydrocarbons and carbon monoxide produced in car exhaust. Engineers are working to produce a device to change these gases into harmless carbon dioxide and water. Japanese scientists are working on a completely new type of petrol-engine designed to produce very low levels of pollutants.

The United States has also passed laws to limit the amount of lead in petrol. Lead is added to make the engine work better, but it produces a great deal of the lead pollution in the air. If the amount of lead is reduced, more petrol will have to be used to produce the same power. Once again, the problem is money. The measures have been postponed because of oil shortages. If oil prices increase, motorists will not willingly spend more money on petrol to make up for the lower lead content. The real answer to automobile pollution is cars powered by steam, electricity or natural gas. But the high cost of developing such vehicles

of the motoring public are likely to hold back development for many years to come.

WATER POLLUTION

Water pollution is almost world-wide. In many ways it is a greater threat than air pollution. The problem of sewage disposal existed long before we started to build factories or drive cars. Drinking water that contains sewage can give rise to diseases such as typhoid and cholera. Water pollution these days is caused mostly by industrial wastes. But sewage is still a problem, as a severe outbreak of cholera in Italy showed in 1973. Many people died in Naples after eating mussels that had grown in water contaminated (made dirty) by the city's sewage.

How Man Spoils His Water

In the 1950s, man-made detergents began to replace soap for washing clothes. Housewives were now able to get their wash cleaner than ever before—but at a cost. These detergents were non-biodegradable; in other words, the bacteria which live in rivers and lakes and normally break down waste materials into natural forms had no effect on them. The foamy detergents remained unchanged in the rivers and streams. Some communities in America found that their drinking water was foamy and bubbly.

A new type of detergent was introduced in the 1960s. This was biodegradable—it could be broken down into waste materials that were useful to other living things. But it contained phosphates, which encouraged the growth of algae —green slimy plants that grow in lakes and rivers. These algae gradually choked up the water courses and—more important—used up the oxygen needed by fish and other forms of wildlife. This over-development of certain types of plant life, called eutrophication, has permanently damaged many lakes all over the world.

As well as detergents, the chemical industries have produced fertilizers, weed-killers and pesticides that have added to the pollution of our waters. New fertilizers have been introduced to help the speedy growth of our food-stuffs. But they eventually flow into rivers and lakes where they increase the amount of destructive algae. New types of weed-killers were introduced at the same time as the detergents. So were pesticides such as DDT, used to control insects and other pests. Both the weed-killers and the pesticides have flowed with the rainwater into large bodies of water. There they have poisoned plant-life, fish, fish-eating birds and people.

Tragedy in Japan

But water pollution can work against us in ways that are more mysterious—and therefore more dangerous. Two of the worst ever cases of water pollution occurred in Japan. Since World War II, Japan has rapidly become industrialized and has suffered most from pollution of all kinds. In 1953 the people of the town of Minimata, now called 'the birthplace of pollution', began to suffer a strange illness. Their bodies started to twitch and they could not walk properly. Some became completely paralysed. Children were born deformed and paralysed. Even the cats and dogs started to behave strangely, staggering drunkenly as they dragged themselves around the streets of the small harbour town.

Doctors finally decided that the cause of all this suffering was mercury poison-

Spraying with pesticides upsets the natural balance of plant and animal communities.

ing. A factory nearby had, for years, been discharging its waste into the bay on which the town of Minimata stands. The fish of the bay collected the mercury in their bodies. When they were eaten by the people and pets of the town, the fish passed on their deadly dose of mercury. The full effect of the poisoning is still not known, but as many as 10,000 people may have been affected in one way or another.

The second case of deadly water pollution occurred near Toyoma, in the north-east of Japan. Near the town are mines, where cadmium is produced for color dyes and steel plating. The air over the town is full of fine particles of cadmium which eventually got into the town's water supply. Since 1962, more than 200 people have been seriously poisoned after drinking this water or eating poisoned rice and soya beans. Many people died with damaged lungs and kidneys.

NEW POLLUTION

As man has built larger factories and found new ways of making his life richer and more enjoyable, so new forms of pollution have sprung up.

Oil is now carried around the world in huge ships which can carry up to 300,000

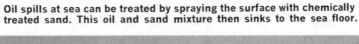
Oil spills at sea can be treated by spraying the surface with chemically treated sand. This oil and sand mixture then sinks to the sea floor.

tons at a time. The English *Globtik Tokyo*, the largest tanker ever built, can carry almost 500,000 tons of oil. But these huge ships are just as likely to sink as smaller ones. When the tanker *Torrey Canyon* ran aground off the coast of England in 1967, it spilled half of its 120,000 tons of oil. Beaches were polluted for miles, and countless fish and sea birds were killed. By today's standards, the *Torrey Canyon* was a small ship.

Nuclear power stations being built in the United States and in Europe will help to produce cheap electricity. But they are a big threat to the world around us. Each nuclear power station produces radio-active waste that is dangerous to all kinds of life. Getting rid of this waste safely is a big problem. Already parts of the Columbia River in the United States are so polluted with radio-active waste that it is dangerous to swim in it.

The two nuclear bombs that were dropped on Japan at the end of World War II killed thousands. Thirty years later, people are still suffering from the after-effects. Today there are power stations which produce as much radio-activity as four of these bombs. By the year 2000 there may be nuclear power stations in Europe and the United States producing nuclear waste as deadly as 1,000 of these bombs each day.

Another type of nuclear activity has caused pollution in the past, but it seems that the problem has been solved for the present. For about 20 years after World War II, the armies of the United States, Britain, France and the Soviet Union tested their new atomic bombs in the atmosphere. This created a type of pollution called nuclear fall-out—a cloud of dangerous radio-active material. It slowly spread over the whole globe and, to a greater or lesser extent, affected everyone in the world. Today all the world's major countries, except France and China, have reached an agreement to end these dangerous open-air tests.

Dangerous Heat

Another form of pollution is less well-known than oil or radio-activity. But it can have equally damaging results to the human and animal populations of the world. This is heat, or thermal, pollution. Many types of factories are responsible for this, but the main culprits are the large new power stations. They take millions of gallons of water for cooling purposes out of rivers and streams, and then send the water back, a few degrees hotter. Rivers that gradually become heated up in this way soon become clogged with algae. They then begin to lose their fish and other forms of wildlife. As bigger factories and power stations are built, the problem of thermal pollution will get worse. Some American scientists have estimated that in less than 30 years, the industry of the United States will be using about a third of the country's fresh water for cooling purposes.

Another, similar problem is the production of carbon dioxide. This gas occurs naturally in the air. It is also produced when things decay and fuels are burned in plentiful supplies of air. Some people believe that because of more industry, motor traffic and aircraft the amount of carbon dioxide in the air is increasing to dangerous levels. Carbon dioxide in large amounts could cause the whole earth to warm up slightly, with disastrous results for the climates of many countries. It may even make the earth's ice-caps melt and flood low-lying areas of the earth, where most of the world's human population lives.